LIGHTER
SIDE
OF THE
LIBRARY

LIGHTER
SIDE
OF THE
LIBRARY

by
JANICE GLOVER

Published By
WILLIAM S. SULLWOLD, PUBLISHING
Taunton, Massachusetts

Library of Congress Catalog Card Number: 74-75520
ISBN 0-88492-003-8

Author's Note

Any book composed of material which has been collected over a period of years, as this one, carries some danger of becoming dated by the time it reaches the reader. I have endeavored to see that this did not happen with the stories and statistics included herein. However, certain trends in the library field should be recognized while reading this book.

Foremost among these is the changing employment situation for professional librarians. As late as 1970 the U. S. Department of Labor was predicting continuing shortages of librarians throughout the decade. But time has shown a shortage of positions instead. Since one reason for compiling this volume was a hope that it would prove helpful in recruiting new librarians, this reversal in the employment scene could lessen the book's impact. However, although we may need fewer librarians, we surely continue to need the very best ones — warm, committed people who know why they want to join the profession and what they are in for. May this book still serve that purpose.

Book titles appearing in ancedotes posed a question. Must they be current? Since bestseller lists change, not only from year to year, but month by month, I decided not to attempt to limit anecdotes to recent titles. Instead, stories incorporating classic or older titles often found in library collections were also included.

As to the library's "image," while still much discussed, a newer word seems to be supplanting it — "outreach." In psychological terms one can liken this to turning from an introverted concern with self to an extroverted concern with others. Yet, just as one has to learn to love and accept oneself before being able to give the best of oneself to others, so "image" inevitably precedes "outreach." When the general public perceives a new image for libraries, outreach will be far more effective.

May 1, 1974.

Contents

Introduction   13

1. Small Patrons   19

2. Further Tales of Small Patrons   29

3. Patrons With Tails   37

4. Teen Tales   43

5. Topsy-Turvy Titles   51

6. Reference   57

7. Please Don't Mumble   73

8. Bookmarks and Overdues   79

9. Merrily We Roll Along   87

10. A Potpourri of Patrons   95

11. Beyond the Call of Duty   105

12. The Girls in the Back Room   113

13. Coffee Break   117

14. A Changing Image   123

Acknowledgments

Without the many generous contributions from librarians and other interested persons, this book surely could not have been written. Those human interest anecdotes which seemed most pertinent were included in the text and came from the following libraries. Grateful acknowledgment is made to each of them.

Maricopa County Free Library, Phoenix, Arizona; Tempe Public Library, Tempe, Arizona.

Barton Library, El Dorado, Arkansas; Clark County Library, Arkadelphia, Arkansas.

Placer County Free Library, Auburn, California; Coronado Public Library, Coronado, California; Fresno County Free Library, San Joaquin Valley Information Service, Fresno, California; Los Angeles Public Library, Los Angeles, California; McHenry Public Library, Modesto, California; Porterville Public Library, Porterville, California.

Pikes Peak Regional District Library, Colorado Springs, Colorado.

The Ansonia Library, Ansonia, Connecticut; Fairfield Public Library, Fairfield, Connecticut; The Ferguson Library, Stamford, Connecticut; New Britain Public Library, New Britain, Connecticut.

Albertson Public Library, Orlando, Florida; Gainesville Public Library, Gainesville, Florida; Jacksonville Free Public Library, Jacksonville, Florida; Miami Public Library, Miami, Florida.

Atlanta Public Library, Atlanta, Georgia.

Library of Hawaii, Honolulu, Hawaii.

Kankakee Public Library, Kankakee, Illinois.

Gary Public Library, Gary, Indiana; Seymour Public Library, Seymour, Indiana.

Public Library of Des Moines, Des Moines, Iowa.

Dodge City Public Library, Dodge City, Kansas; Topeka Public Library, Topeka, Kansas; Wichita City Library, Wichita, Kansas.

Shreve Memorial Library, Shreveport, Louisiana.

Bangor Public Library, Bangor, Maine; Lewiston Public Library, Lewiston, Maine.

Gale Free Library, Holden, Massachusetts; Hyannis Public Library, Hyannis, Massachusetts; Millicent Public Library, Fairhaven, Massachusetts; Osterville Free Library, Osterville, Massachusetts; State Regional Library Center, North Reading, Massachusetts; State Regional Library Center, Pittsfield, Massachusetts; Wellesley Free Public Library, Wellesley, Massachusetts.

Kalamazoo Public Library, Kalamazoo, Michigan.

Hibbing Public Library, Hibbing, Minnesota.

Free Public Library, Hannibal, Missouri; Missouri State Library, Jefferson City, Missouri; St. Louis Public Library, St. Louis, Missouri.

The City Library, Manchester, New Hampshire.

Gallup Public Library, Gallup, New Mexico; Santa Fe Public Library, Santa Fe, New Mexico.

Seymour Library, Auburn, New York; Mount Vernon Public Library, Mount Vernon, New York; The New York Public Library, New York, New York; Utica Public Library, Utica, New York.

Charlotte and Mecklenburg County Library, Charlotte, North Carolina; Wilmington Public Library, Wilmington, North Carolina.

Veterans Memorial Public Library, Bismarck, North Dakota; Grand Forks Public Library, Grand Forks, North Dakota.

Bowling Green Public Library, Bowling Green, Ohio; Columbus Public Library, Columbus, Ohio; Dayton and Montgomery County Library, Dayton, Ohio; Findlay Public Library, Findlay, Ohio; Garfield Heights Library, Garfield Heights, Ohio; Lane Public Library, Hamilton, Ohio; Toledo Public Library, Toledo, Ohio.

Oklahoma City Libraries, Oklahoma City, Oklahoma.

Klamath County Library, Klamath Falls, Oregon.

Carnegie Library of Pittsburgh, Pittsburgh, Pennsylvania; Reading Public Library, Reading, Pennsylvania.

Anderson County Library, Anderson, South Carolina; Orangeburg County Free Library, Orangeburg, South Carolina.

Mary E. Bivins Memorial Library, Amarillo, Texas; Austin Public Library, Austin, Texas; Ector County Library, Odessa, Texas.

Carnegie Free Library, Ogden, Utah.

Fletcher Free Library, Burlington, Vermont; Rutland Free Library, Rutland, Vermont; St. Johnsbury Athenaeum, St. Johnsbury, Vermont.

Jones Memorial Library, Lynchburg, Virginia; Richmond Public Library, Richmond, Virginia.

Everett Public Library, Everett, Washington.

Morgantown Public Library, Morgantown, West Virginia.

Eau Claire Public Library, Eau Claire, Wisconsin; Boys' and Girls' Library, Kenosha, Wisconsin; Madison Public Library, Madison, Wisconsin.

Natrona County Public Library, Casper, Wyoming.

Calgary Public Library, Calgary, Alberta, Canada; Edmonton Public Library, Edmonton, Alberta, Canada; Ottawa Public Library, Ottawa, Ontario, Canada; Vancouver Public Library, Vancouver, British Columbia, Canada.

Palmerston Public Library, Palmerston, New Zealand.

In addition to the above mentioned libraries, several individuals should be thanked for special information and help. Miss M. Jane Manthorne, Coordinator of Young Adult Services at Boston Public Library and Miss Lillian Morrison, Assistant Coordinator of Young Adult Services at The New York Public Library were of special assistance in writing "Teen Tales."

Mrs. Martha Healey, Head, Extension Services, Washington County Free Library, Hagerstown, Maryland and Mr. A. W. Baehr, Sales Manager, The Gerstenslager Company, Wooster, Ohio supplied information for "Merrily We Roll Along."

Mrs. Norma Hawkins, Assistant Librarian at the Kitsilano Branch of the Vancouver Public Library gave permission to quote from her article "Liberry Teachers" which appeared in *Viewpoints*, Vancouver Public Library staff publication.

Also, a number of newspapers and other publications must be given credit for material used. They are:

Toledo Blade, Toledo, Ohio; *Colorado Springs Free Press*, Colorado Springs, Colorado; *Gaylords' Triangle*, Gaylord Bros., Inc., Syracuse, New York (Library supplies); *Pittsburgh Post-Gazette*, Pittsburgh, Pennsylvania; *Salt Lake City Deseret News*, Salt Lake City, Utah; and *Shreveport Times*, Shreveport, Louisiana.

The pamphlet *Parnassus Junior* by Marianne Brish, printed by "A Friend of the Washington County Free Library, Hagerstown, Maryland, and "reprinted from *Randolph-Macon Prose and Verse*, Volume III, (1951), Randolph-Macon Woman's College, Lynchburg, Virginia," furnished extensive material and quotes for "Merrily We Roll Along."

Introduction

Too many people still think of the Public Library as Dullsville. Oh perhaps, if they stop to consider it, they may concede it has its good points. For children needing additional information to complete homework, it's fine. For little old ladies, the kind who enjoy love stories but whose sensibilities are shocked by modern novels, there will be, perhaps, yellow-paged romances written long ago. For the head-in-the-clouds intellectual, for him they may agree, the library holds a great fund of material.

But just try to tell Mr. and Mrs. Everybody that their Public Library can be an attractive, lively community center, staffed with librarians who are courteous, warm, interested, and capable of displaying, on appropriate occasions, a sense of humor, and the response from non-library or casual users is likely to be: "Come now, who do you think you're kidding!"

Rude reactions such as this do not come alone from the uneducated or the non-reader. Several years ago *Time* magazine queried 1,666 of its employees on their attitudes toward libraries and librarians. While a limited survey of this sort cannot be taken too seriously, the answers received from presumably intelligent, literate persons were, on the whole, not very flattering. Among the more critical pre-selected statements with which *Time* employees agreed were that libraries were "not conveniently located," were "physically unattractive," "had a poor selection of books." When asked to write a brief description of a typical librarian, some granted that she might be "intelligent, patient, dedicated, neat, quiet, cultured, hard-working." But other, less complimentary adjectives were also used: "old maid, humorless, unimaginative, dowdy, colorless, opinionated, inhibited, and naive."

It must be admitted that some libraries and librarians probably do fit this dismal picture. After all, in the United States alone there are approximately 13,000 public libraries (including branches) and about 106,000 professional librarians (employed in all types of libraries), so it is not surprising that some drab buildings and misfit employees would be included. No large segment of society is perfect. But, for the most part, the popular but thoughtless, disparaging image of libraries is a terribly distorted one.

This greatly concerns librarians. *What the Public Thinks of the Library* ranks high as a perennial theme for disucssion at local, state, regional, and national library gatherings. But as yet, to judge from a conversation overheard by a librarian attending a California Library Association meeting, not much progress has been made in acquainting the general public with the true nature of library work.

This particular librarian was eating at the counter in the Coffee Shop of the Hotel Senator in Sacramento, which was headquarters for the California Library Association meeting, when two men came in and sat down beside her. From their talk she gathered that they were legislators from the Capitol. Then she heard the word "librarians" and was all ears.

Mr. A:	"I hear that the librarians are in town for a convention."
Mr. B:	"Yes, and they don't seem to be as rowdy as the usual crowd. They're to be here four days I understand."
Mr. A:	"What in the world would they have to talk about all that time?" Then, answering his own question, "They probably read books and tell each other about them."
Mr. B:	(Very kindly) "Well, they must have their troubles, too!"

Indeed they do — one of the major ones being to change that old image!

Writers of library literature must take some of the blame for creating a lackluster picture. Many fine technical volumes have been written for librarians, and occasionally — usually during National Library Week — popularized articles about the library appear in newspapers and magazines. But precious little has found its way into general print which depicts the human, everyday events which occur in libraries.

It was in an attempt to fill this void that I undertook to collect and compile a book on the lighter side of the library.

A second motivating reason was more personal. Several years ago a friend disputed a statement I made that "Library work, far from being a dull, dusty occupation, is frequently composed of elements of humor, drama, and glamour." I wanted to prove to her and to others of like mind that this really was so.

Examples in all three categories came from many libraries. Fitting the drama classification was this contribution from a Pennsylvania librarian.

"The best stories in libraries are not always sweetness and light. The most unforgettable character in my book was a voluptuous blonde who came in clad in the scantiest shorts and halter that were probably ever seen inside a library. She needed a book about poisons — quick — because her husband was trying to poison her, and she was in a hurry because he was double-parked outside. A great spot for James Bond," observed the librarian, "But I'm not he, so I never found out what happened next. And that's the way it is with many library stories."

Another little drama with a more predictable ending was enacted in a West Virginia library.

A young man rushed into the library at 8:30 one evening and asked, "Do you have a copy of a medical book?"

Not able to locate the one she wanted on the shelf, the librarian took a little longer to search for it and went into the room where book mending was done. All the while the young man was shifting impatiently from one foot to the other. Finally he could not stand it a minute longer.

"Will you please hurry, M'am. My wife is expecting and we want to know if her time has come!"

Quickly the librarian found him a medical book with the appropriate information and wished him Godspeed.

As for glamour, few places provide better showcases for celebrities than libraries. Many of today's books are authored by, or at least carry the byline of, noted statesmen, explorers, actors, and television personalities. Such individuals are often invited to speak at special programs arranged by libraries. In addition, experts in many fields are asked to discuss and demonstrate their skills for younger patrons. For instance, included in a Summer Festival put on by the Free Public Library of New Bedford, Massachusetts, were a skin diver, a magician, a folk-singer, and an expert in the art of paper-folding (origami).

Glamour of a different sort — possibly intellectual excitement better expresses it — comes to those librarians who help authors find material for works in progress. It is a pleasure to meet creative, lively-minded individuals. Beyond that, when the particular book or article is published, or the television script aired, there is bound to be some ego satisfaction in knowing you have played a small part in making it what it is.

So, as you can see, "dramatic" and "glamorous" events do take place in libraries. Still, it must be admitted, they happen only on occasion. In contrast, humorous incidents are practically a daily occurrence. Ample testimony to this fact is given in the large number of replies I received to a request for library anecdotes.

Letters explaining the purpose of this book were sent to 375 librarians in all fifty states and nine Canadian Provinces. About one-third replied. Many correspondents were enthusiastic and generous too. Where I had asked if they would contribute an anecdote or two, quite a few sent pages of incidents, often apologizing because they could not remember more. In my letters, I pointed out that there could be no recompense, that choices between stories would be made and editing done, and that submission of material to me would indicate permission to publish unless they stated otherwise. Most anecdotes received had not appeared elsewhere, although a few were from staff publications or newspaper feature articles.

As to compensation, one librarian wrote: "Believe me, prizes are not in order. It will be reward enough to have someone rise to our defense in a way which can do more good than all the recruiting efforts and National Library Week programs yet devised."

Because some libraries wished to remain anonymous and others hoped for publicity, a ruling on credits had to be made. When queried about this, I explained that I would mention the library where it was essential to the sense of the story, but most of the time only a state or region would be given, and often no geographical designation at all. (Contributors not requesting otherwise are listed in the *Acknowledgments* section.) The decision to avoid specific labels was not made solely because I wished to be legally prudent. The more stories I read, the more evident it became that libraries — the people who work in them and the people who patronize them — share pretty universal experiences.

One example: Similar anecdotes about librarians hunting for books on "Youth in Asia" when what was wanted was material on the subject of euthanasia ("the practice of painlessly putting to death people suffering from incurable and distressing diseases") came from such widely separated places as Ottawa, Ontario; Findlay, Ohio; Los Angeles, California; Reading, Pennsylvania; Casper, Wyoming; and Palmerston, New Zealand. (This last from a foreign librarian visiting the Seattle, Washington, Public Library.)

All the preceding conditions were cheerfully agreed to by most librarians. Typical comments were that they were delighted to have "the opportunity of immortalizing the funny things which happen on the job" and "Please feel free to change them (the anecdotes) in any way you like."

The majority point of view was well expressed by Josephine B. Farrington, former Chief, Public Relations Department, St. Louis Public Library, St. Louis, Missouri.

"We appreciate your efforts," she said, "to do away with that age-old and erroneous image of the librarian with the flat shoes, horn-rimmed glasses, hair in a bun, saying 'Sh-sh-sh!' Somehow she dies hard. On television they use this type and it always burns us up. So we hope your book is a tremendous success and gives the great American public the idea that modern librarians are human beings with a sense of humor, a love of people and books, and an appreciation of the fun things in life."

May what follows give all readers — not just librarians — entertainment as well as enlightenment about some of the behind-the-scenes doings in libraries.

Chapter One

Small Patrons

Where shall we start to view the funnier facets of libraries? Probably the best place to begin is where the majority of borrowers do — as small patrons in the Children's Department.

Visits to the library start at a tender age. It's not unusual to see librarians performing baby-holding services for browsing mothers. If the initial encounter between infant and librarian is pleasant, one can assume that the little twig will be bent in the proper direction, toward good reading in years to come. But if the librarian is not adept at baby-bouncing or strongly protests at having her glasses snatched, wails and woe may ensue. It's even possible this first unpleasant library experience could so mark the baby that — horrible thought — as he grows older he will prefer to gain his knowledge from television rather than books! Suggestions: bone up on babies; keep a few toys at the charging desk; or tell Mother you're sorry but you just sprained your wrist and cannot hold her dimpled darling.

The record for the youngest declared patron could go to a boy I once encountered. He had checked out a book on infinity and we were discussing whether or not it was too old for him.

"I'm going into the fourth grade in September," he announced as though that settled it. Then peering at me through his glasses, he queried, "How long have you been here?"

"Just this summer," I answered, deciding not to confuse the issue with a long list of previously held positions.

"I thought you were new." This no doubt explained my misgivings about his ability to comprehend infinity. "Well, I've been coming here a long time," he went on. "Ever since I was pregnant." Seeing my slightly startled expression, he amended, "I mean ever since I was two months pregnant inside my mother."

Toddlers, although sometimes brought by older brothers and sisters, are usually accompanied by Mother or Daddy on the first excursion to their own special library world — the Children's Room. For a little tot, more sophisticated about supermarkets and restaurants than libraries, this first experience can be bewildering.

One small girl, tightly grasping her mother's hand, stared at two round reading tables which had been stripped bare of books by earlier eager young patrons. Then she asked, "Mummy, where are the dishes?"

Usually it takes but a few minutes before these 2 or 3-year-olds on their first visit to the Children's Room are happily pulling picture books from the shelves. "I want a book, Mummy," they plead. "Buy me a book." "Liberry" is a word soon added to their vocabulary. *"Free* Public" is a lot harder to understand.

Once convinced by Mother that they may take a book home, the smallest patron is reluctant to give up the new-found treasure. It requires all the smiling persuasion the librarian can summon to be allowed to take the book away long enough to charge it. That accomplished, off goes the small one, hugging a book half as big as he is.

Registration rules for small patrons vary. Some libraries require that a child be old enough to print his name before being issued a card. The growing tendency is to let a child have his own borrower's card as soon as he is interested in looking at books and can handle them fairly carefully.

While it is always possible to borrow tiny tot's books on the card of a parent or brother or sister, there is something very special about having a card of one's own. It's a sort of status symbol for the very young which causes eyes to shine and voices to exclaim gleefully, "Hey, I'm getting a library card!"

Requests for registration cards come in many forms.

"I want to enlist."

"I wantta sign myself up."

And I once had a small boy come up to me and say, with a slightly toothless grin, "I want a thicket." This required double translation — thicket to ticket, ticket to registration card.

All the foregoing requests have an unmistakable masculine ring to them. But only a small, blonde feminine charmer could have asked for "a little biddy baby library card." She, it turned out, had just celebrated her fourth birthday.

Desirable as it is to receive a library card, making out the registration sometimes poses problems. A little boy applying for his card could not remember his father's first name.

Trying to be helpful, the librarian asked, "What does your Mother call your Daddy?"

"Oh," he smiled with relief, "Honey."

Library rules for alphabetical filing of borrower's cards, last name first, can cause confusion. "Wouldn't you think," said one young miss upon looking at her borrower's card for the first time, "that the library would know better than to write my name backwards."

Possession of a first library card is a proud moment for most children, but pride sometimes goeth before a fall. At an Ohio library where I worked this turned out to be literally true. In the summer the library, with its reading club and story hours, shared popularity with the outdoor swimming pool next door. It was a generally happy relationship. Library cards were left on the way to the pool and collected later along with a book or two. Most young patrons had dried beyond the drippy stage by the time they reached the library. But there were occasional mishaps. One morning a boy handed me a soggy card and explained cheerfully: "I fell in the pool and my card went with me."

Some youngsters with painful memories of long lists of articles lost over the years — mittens, rubbers, report cards, to name but a few — are fearful that they will misplace their library card as well. Upon applying for her card, a 9-year-old girl asked the Children's Librarian, "Could I have another card in case I lose this one? I don't want to write out another prescription."

While applying for a duplicate registration card to replace one lost, a young girl studied the form line marked "Last seen on or about . . . " (To be filled with a date.) Then she completed it with " . . . my dresser."

Borrower's cards, even when not lost, can become tattered and torn. This appears to be especially true when they reside in small boys' pockets along with assortments of marbles, nails, and maybe a baby toad or small snake. A Connecticut librarian tells of a boy who handed her his torn card with the plea, "Please, Miss, will you hitch up my card?"

And a small Southern lad, presenting a very torn, dirty card to the Children's Librarian, asked, "Which day of the week do you come to the library to get your library card cleaned?"

At this same library another boy, apparently aware of local levies, inquired apprehensively as he handed the librarian a dime for a new card, "Is there a tax on this?"

Perhaps the best definition of what a library card can mean was voiced, quite unintentionally, by a boy who presented an expired card. "My old one's inspired," he explained. Would that all borrower's cards issued to children be considered as inspired tickets to joy and adventure!

Pre-school Story Hour is a big event for the smallest patrons. Into the Children's Room they flock, some clutching dolls and toys, chattering in highpitched voices. Sometimes a pre-kindergartener, awed by the sight of so many children, clings desperately to Mother's hand and cries as she leaves. If sobs crescendo into screams, he may have to be rescued and returned to her care with the diplomatic suggestion that perhaps he will enjoy story-telling more when he is a bit older. You never, no never, state that if you have to out-yell him through an entire story-telling session, you will end up with a bad case of laryngitis and probably several sympathetic sobbers who join in on his act.

Even happy chatterers take some calming before the main event can commence. One librarian likened trying to quiet her children down in order to begin story-telling to making a plaster cast out of a breaking wave!

One young man seemed to confuse Story Hour with going to the movies. "Hey," he demanded, "where do you sell the popcorn?"

Sticky fingers and books do not make an ideal combination. Even so, some libraries distribute candy or simple refreshments at special Story Hours such as those held around Christmas time and at Halloween.

A Canadian librarian tells of a Halloween incident which happened to her. Halloween ghost stories had been promised for Story Hour at her library. Lights were turned out and the auditorium decorated with jack o' lanterns and a life-size "ghost". Dimness made an eerie atmosphere. But her style was somewhat cramped by an earnest-looking redhead with her small brother by the hand. "Please don't tell any stories that are exciting," she pleaded, "because if you do Johnnie will wet his pants."

Christmas is a joyous season — a very special one for many children. Fortunately for the story-telling librarian, there is a wealth of Christmas literature, both sacred and secular, from which she may choose. Yet for little people, the traditional often gets scrambled with the more trite.

A librarian in New Mexico tells this one. A few days before Christmas she read the poem *'Twas the Night Before Christmas* to her group. They were attentive, wide-eyed, and excited at the vision of Santa Claus and his reindeer. Then, after she finished reading, a little boy with a most puzzled look on his face piped up, "And where was Rudolph the Red-Nosed Reindeer?"

In South Carolina, children were listening to a story about a birthday party.

When the librarian had finished she asked, "Will any of you be having a birthday soon?"

Several children volunteered the date of their birthdays, but one little boy said he didn't know when his birthday was.

"Well, Greg," queried the librarian, "why don't you learn when your birthday comes?"

"Because," he explained, "I want it to be a surprise to me when it does come."

The importance one small feminine patron attached to Story Hour is indicated by the following incident. A tiny, jeans-clad girl, who lived next door to a country library, stopped her play as the Children's Librarian drove into the library yard one day. Eagerly she climbed the fence which separated her home from the library to greet her friend, for friend the librarian had become since the little girl started attending pre-school Story Hour each Friday morning.

As cheery "Hi's" were being exchanged, the little girl heard her Mother calling her.

"Bye, now," the youngster called as she climbed down from the fence. "I'll see you Friday morning with my dress on."

Many libraries regularly schedule visits from school classes. Such expeditions, although instructive and worthwhile, can become chaotic. Feet, frequently muddy, tramp loudly; books are snatched from shelves willy-nilly and replaced in the most unlikely spots; and the librarian can usually count on at least one card being torn from the catalog file and brought to her with the request "this is the book I want" before she has a chance to explain the niceties of using the catalog.

Small wonder that a librarian's feelings sometimes surface despite her best intentions. A certain librarian, planning to bid a touring kindergarten group good-bye with the words, "I'm delighted to have had you come, and before you go . . . " was amazed to hear herself say instead, "I'm delighted to have you go!"

Despite sighs of relief which sometimes follow exit of the thundering herd, positive results do come from such visits. First to appear are those letters which teachers customarily require pupils to write to the librarian, thanking her for their guided tour. Quite a few librarians collect them. Here are some:

Dear Miss E . . .

Thank you for showing us how to use the file. Your talk was more intresting (sic) than last year's . . .

Sincerely,
John L.

Dear Miss R . . .

Thank you for telling me how to use the file because I never knew how to use a file and I am glad that you did because I am going to the library next week to get a book. Who knows I might just use the file.

Yours truly,
Robert D.

Dear Mrs. H . . .

Thank you for showing us the library. I enjoyed the tour almost better than baseball.

Sincerely,
Allan S.

A male librarian informs us that after a class tours his library, he usually follows with a bit of story-telling and then goes into the care and handling of books borrowed from the library. One time he apparently overstressed the idea of keeping the books clean. "Children should protect library books and should not let them get dirty like this one (book shown at that point). "We should never let books fall into the mud, etc." Within two or three days after the trip, he began to receive little notes written on large yellow lined sheets. The one which most impressed him went like this:

Dear Mr. M . . .

I liked your library. I liked you.

I liked your pretty librarian. You were a nice librarian even if you were a man.

I liked the big books. I liked all the books.

I even liked the dirty books.

Love,
Jennie, Grade 1

With such enthusiastic letters, what librarian can complain about the straightening-up sessions which follow tours? The cherry which tops off the cream of flattering letters arrives at the moment when you observe some small patron, recently initiated into the mysteries of the card file, proudly show another child how to look up — and find — a desired book.

Automated systems of charging books, employed now by most middle-sized and large libraries, fascinate children. For that matter, the simple ink pad and stamp dater still used by some small libraries has its attractions too. It's almost impossible to keep little tots from smearing fingers or tattooing hands with FREE PUBLIC LIBRARY and the due date. The older child, however, is mechanically minded. He wants to know exactly how the Gaylord, Brodac, or other make charging machine works. The Regiscope Photo/Charger held real magic for one boy. "Please turn it on," he pleaded. "I want to watch it make books."

One library which uses a charging machine reports that its young patrons are not above borrowing each other's cards. A certain young man had just presented a card marked "Robert" when he was greeted by a passing friend as "Tom". Unabashed, he explained to the librarian, "That's my maiden name."

Like other marvels of this automated age, charging machines can be temperamental. If a bent or ragged book card is too forcibly inserted in the slot, it sometimes catches. Instead of a smart click and an easily withdrawn card, the machine holds the card and produces a loud, angry groaning sound which can be heard for some distance. This happened as an 8-year-old boy was checking out a book. His face became very serious, and he appeared on the verge of tears as he asked, "Does that mean I owe a FINE?"

Although he did not, small patrons do pay their share of fines on overdue books. Tardy borrowers often express their concern in unusual terms.

"I took this book and I overdued it."

"I'm sorry but my book is overdone."

"Please reduce this book. I want it again."

Asking to have a book renewed so it would not become overdue, one little girl said she would like to expire her book for another two weeks. Quite likely she'd heard her mother ask to have books extended. This request, incidentally, always brings to mind visions of a short, thick book being rolled into elongated shape like so much dough.

26

Paying fines often brings distress, especially when a portion of the child's own allowance is involved.

One little girl, fighting with her older sister who had just paid a five cent fine, cried, "Hey, Mommy didn't give you that money to buy a book!"

And a small boy, returning two books which were a day overdue, but having no money, laid a big red apple on the librarian's desk and asked hesitantly, "Do you want an apple?"

Young patrons — and not-so-young ones, too — have a rather hazy idea of where fine money ultimately goes. At a Wisconsin library, one of the librarians had recently bought a fine new car. This shining bus, parked outside the library, was much admired and discussed by a group of young borrowers. A few days after its appearance, one of these boys had a big fine to pay on overdue books. As he laid his money on the desk, he remarked, "Now we know how you got that new car!"

During the summer months many libraries conduct Vacation Reading Clubs. No special pressure is put upon children to join these, but most wish to. The summer reader, unlike some of the school-year patrons, generally comes to the library because he enjoys books. He would read anyway — Club or not. But the Club makes the whole thing more fun, as well as improving his appreciation of literature.

However, some librarians do not fully approve of the idea. They feel that too much stress on competition and winning a prize (usually a book) for reading the most volumes can mean careless quantity reading rather than careful quality reading.

Yet, if the staff in the Children's Room can give adequate time to assisting in book selection and listening to or reading book reports, it can be a pleasant project for all concerned. Certainly a librarian gets to know her small patrons individually as she seldom can during the more hectic school year. And she has an opportunity to help both the slow and the advanced reader.

One little girl, member of a Vacation Reading Club, was obviously having trouble writing her report. She paused, pencil poised above paper, to ask, "Mrs. Smith, how do you spell 'druther'?"

"Druther?" asked the puzzled librarian.

"Yes. Like I'd druther ride a horse than play ball."

Then there was the precocious young reader — small for his age and just leaving the fourth grade — who scornfully rejected his mother's suggestion that he join the Reading Club. "They'll probably think I should be reading *The Three Bears*," he objected.

The Children's Librarian approached him warily and after conversing with him discovered that he had just finished reading *Land of the Pharaohs* and Guerber's *Story of the Roman People*. When she handed him *The Odyssey, The Iliad*, and Jessup's *Wonderful World of Archaeology*, he quickly changed his mind about joining the Reading Club.

To his mother's comment that he knew more about ancient history than she did, he added confidentially to the librarian, "Yes, SHE didn't even know who was the Roman Consul at the time of the Carthaginian Wars. It was Regulus, you know."

"P.S.," wrote the librarian who sent this story, "We didn't but we didn't admit to such ignorance!"

Chapter Two

Further Tales of Small Patrons

A certain pediatrician prescribes at least one book a month, along with proper diet and vitamins, for all his young patients. He explains that he wants to be sure they develop their imaginations as well as their bodies.

This is a commendable aim, but any Children's Librarian could tell him that imagination in the average child is about as difficult to suppress as spots in a case of measles.

Such imagination often pops out in unexpected ways. There was, for instance, the little girl who entered a Missouri library and noticed that there were not as many books on the shelves as usual. "My," she observed, "the library must have gone on a diet. It looks thinner."

(Speaking of diets, a 10-year-old girl requested "a book of exercises to trim my stomach down.")

In another Missouri library, a branch librarian was feeling discouraged that all her efforts to refurnish and rearrange the library were going unnoticed. Her morale received a boost when a tiny girl came up to her and commented, "Thank you for the comfort of the library."

General decor was what this young lady had in mind, but two small boys were more interested in essential equipment. In obvious distress, they asked the librarian of a small branch library, "Miss, can we use the toilet?"

"Sorry, we have no public toilet."

In unison the boys replied, "But we're not public, we're Catholic!"

I often feel that the smallest patrons should be labeled the Dr. Seuss set. So popular are the nonsense tales written under this pseudonym that most pre-school children demand to take out every book written by this author. Despite the disapproving clucks of some critics as to their literary quality, and the emotions of baffled parents who try to read sense into something which was never intended to make sense, 4 to 6-year-olds love Dr. Suess. Remembering titles previously read is something of a problem, though.

One little boy who had been taking books since he was 2 approached the librarian.

"Do you got (he always said "got") a Dr. Seuss that's about gooey stuff?"

After a moment's puzzlement the librarian successfully produced *Scrambled Eggs Super.*

And then there was the kindergartener who when asked, "Who took out your tonsils?" replied, "I don't know, but I'm pretty sure it wasn't Dr. Seuss."

One of the appealing things about this Dr. Suess set is their eagerness to share the delights of the picture book with the librarian. One small boy brought a book to the librarian's desk to show her a picture of a large swamp.

"Oh," she observed, "I'll bet there are snakes and frogs in that swamp."

"Yes," he agreed, "and alligators and snapdragons, too."

Another charming tête-à-tête took place between a bookmobile librarian and a young lad who had a generous sprinkling of freckles on his face.

"Jimmy, where did all those freckles come from?" asked the librarian.

"The angels kissed me."

"You're so cute I could kiss you myself," exclaimed the attractive young librarian.

"Oh, no!" he replied emphatically. "You're no angel!"

Small patrons frequently have unusual ideas about what goes on behind the scenes in a library. Two little girls, walking past the open door of a work room, stopped to watch several assistants typing.

"What are they doing?" asked the first child.

"Oh," replied the second, "they are writing books to put on the shelves."

And there was the little boy who demanded to know of a Children's Librarian, "Where is the People's Department?" Seems Mama was a "people" and he'd lost her there. (The Adult Department.)

A Connecticut librarian reports overhearing the following remark. Two small girls were walking past the library when one, evidently a regular patron, pointed out the Children's Room to her non-borrowing friend. "There's a lady in there," she explained in wonderment, "who believes in fairies."

As a special treat on her birthday, a Midwestern Children's Librarian gave the youngsters a stick of gum as they checked their books. She later overheard two of the children discussing her birthday and wondering how old she was.

One little girl said, "I think she is about as old as my Mother."

Her friend replied, "She couldn't be, she's not even married!"

Should anyone have the impression that library work is always routine and predictable, let them sit for one day in the seat of any Children's Librarian. Across the desk will flow such an amazing hodgepodge of requests that, to answer them, one must be a combination of all-wise oracle, sleuthing Sherlock Holmes, and understanding psychologist. Above all, the Children's Librarian must have that subtle sixth sense which tells her when to join in a chuckle or suppress it to fit the serious purpose of a child.

Here are a few of the surprising requests received by Children's Librarians.

One evening a pre-school lad, accompanied by his parents, asked a librarian for "The story of the boy who vomited the ribbon."

"We don't have a story like that," replied the puzzled librarian.

"Oh, yes you do!" insisted the small boy.

"Where?" he was asked.

He ran to a shelf and in triumph pulled out *'Twas the Night Before Christmas.* Why?

(Answer)

"Away to the window
I flew like a flash,
Tore open the shutters
And *threw up the sash.*"

When a very young gentleman asked for a book on how to tie knots, he was handed a pamphlet, "Knots and How To Tie Them."

"No," he exclaimed, "I want to know how to tie my tie!"

A little girl asked for a dictionary of a cinnamon (synonyms).

"I want a book about how to make a catapult," requested an 8-year-old boy.

After looking through several books on the Middle Ages and weapons, the librarian located a big, clear picture of a catapult. "Will this do?" she asked. "It's the nearest we have."

"It'll do fine," he replied. "And, oh boy, are those neighbors going to be sorry they kicked my dog!"

Then there was the boy who renewed a book titled *What's Inside of Me?*

"Reading that book just makes me sick," he confided to the librarian.

This caused another boy standing nearby to put in an eager request. "Let me have that book next. I'd like to read it and get sick — then no school."

Request received by a Florida library: "I would like an experiment with a volcano."

Four fourth grade boys appeared at a Children's Librarian's desk. One ventured the question, quite meekly, "Do you have any books on 'tention?"

Interpreting this as "attention" and thinking he and his friends might desire to do a little better in school, the librarian asked, "Do you mean studying, something to help you in school, or manners?"

"No," emphatically. "We want a book on — you know — AT-TEN-SHUN, that army stuff!"

The librarian produced a book on marching from the adult collection and *West Point* by Engeman. This seemed to satisfy the boys, and after studying the books for a while they lined up at the door with the leader calling "ATTENTION" as they marched out.

A shy little girl sidled up to the librarian's desk. "Is the author of *Little Women* in?" she asked.

An 8-year-old boy asked if a Florida library had a book which contained Sir Winston Churchill's speeches.

"I will have to be making speeches," he explained proudly. "You see, I've just been elected President of the third grade."

And then there were two small girls who came into an Ohio library, their arms twined about one another. "We," they informed the librarian, "would like some third grade books on love."

★ ★ ★

Some libraries own facsimile of famous historical documents, such as the Declaration of Independence, which are framed and hung in prominent positions. Too often, however, they become so much a part of the decorative background that neither librarians nor patrons really see them, any more than they would the average picture. But this was evidently not the case with one fourth grader. He stood at his older sister's elbow as she telephoned their mother to report on progress being made in their excursion to the library.

"Let me talk to Mom," he interrupted. "Mom, I think I'm going to have trouble with that *Gettysburg Address*." (Pause) "No, the library has it all right, but I can't read Lincoln's writing."

When their help is sought, Children's Librarians are usually adept at matching the right book with the right child. But sometimes a child wants a book which the librarian doubts will fill his needs or interest him. Even so, she may feel it better to let him find this out himself rather than her being argumentive and negative about the whole book-choosing process.

Being human, however, it was probably with some difficulty that one librarian refrained from saying, "I told you so," when a third grade boy returned a large adult book on airplanes against which she had counseled. He slammed it on her desk with the disgusted remark, "This tells me more about airplanes than I wanted to know."

★ ★ ★

Something which adults often fail to understand is the strong attachment a child can develop for a specific book.

A parent in an Ohio library looked more closely at books her child was checking out and protested, "But, John, you have TWO books just alike! Oh, for goodness sake, these two are just like the one you already have at school! Whatever are you thinking of to want THREE copies of the same book?"

"It's my favorite," replied John. "I read the one at school two times already, and I'll read these two times each, too."

Such an explanation might seem confusing to adults, but it appears quite logical to children, if the number of similar incidents reported by librarians is any criterion. For instance, an Arkansas librarian told of a small girl who came to the checkout machine with two identical books. When it was explained to her that the books were exactly alike, she said, "Oh yes, I know. You see, I want to read it twice!"

A slightly different reason was given to me by two young girls who chose identical titles. They looked at me as if they thought I were not quite bright when I drew this fact to their attention. "But we always read the same books," they declared. And indeed they often did — in school. Who can say that simultaneous silent reading may not strengthen a friendship, while at the same time it brings understanding of fictional characters? A book may mean different things to different children. The independent, adventurous child may prefer to step into the world of fact and fiction alone. But a child who feels more secure with other humans than with the printed word may grow into the joys of reading by sharing his early book experiences with another child.

Children's Librarians say they carry on active lost and found departments. Included among the lost are such items as single mittens, baseball caps which are still around in football season, rubbers, and assorted school papers — with and without stars. This service appears to cover, not only inanimate objects, but persons as well.

In a Florida library the Children's Librarian was somewhat perplexed by the description supplied by a small girl who had planned to meet her friend in the library "right after school."

"Well," the worried child explained, "she has hair not too long and is a little bit bigger than me, but still she might be a little smaller instead. I'm not sure whether it was her blue or her pink dress she was wearing today, but it was one of them. She was supposed to meet me here, and I don't see her so has she already left?"

Fortunately for all concerned the friend made a timely entrance and everyone was satisfied.

After making class tours of their library, youngsters often write notes of appreciation to librarians. At least one library, the Carnegie Library of Pittsburgh, Pennsylvania, carried this process a step further. Children from grades one through eight were invited to write on the subject "what the library means to me." Over 1,000 letters were received. After being carefully judged, those considered outstanding appeared in an article in the *Pittsburgh Post-Gazette* just prior to National Library Week. Responses were varied, to say the least. Here are a few.

"I like your library. I like to learn new words. And boy do I learn them . . . " B. H., Age 6

"It contains the most valuable information in the world . . . Reading a book about artifacul respration (sic) may come in handy at a time of danger . . . " N.S., Age 11

"I think it is fun to see books all in a row. Next to Washington, D.C., Virginia and Gettysburgh (sic), the library is the best place to go . . . " K. G., Age 10

"Will you put a Daniel Boone book in the library. And I will come to the library and look at the Daniel Boone book . . . " D. T., Second Grade

"You can pick any book you want. And I like the girls that check the books . . . " L. C., Age 8

"You are putting traveling thoughts into my mind. One day I told my mother that I was going to New York. She asked me how? I said wait and see. To the library I went. I brought home a book on the city of New York. She really was surprised . . . " R. P., Age 9

"It is the one place where I can really relax and get away from all the hussull and bussull (sic) of the fast-moving world . . . " J. R., Age 13

"I think of the wonderful sounds in the Library . . . did you ever hear it? I notice the nothing noise that fills the air. Mabey (sic) the breathing of a person, the turning of pages . . . " M.S., Age 13

Which makes one wonder if perhaps librarians have not gone too far in trying to make modern libraries informal, conversation-allowed centers of activity. Important as it is to provide stimulating library-related projects, the old hush-hush atmosphere, strictly enforced, had something in its favor. We may not realize how highly some young patrons prize "the nothing noise that fills the air" in libraries, the delightful oasis a quiet, calm place can be in "the hussull and bussull of the fast-moving world."

Chapter Three

Patrons With Tails

"The best way to increase circulation in the children's department would be to install a small zoo," observes Norma Hawkins of the Kitsalano Branch of the Vancouver, British Columbia, public library system.

There's no doubt that exhibits of animals, fish, or birds are an extra drawing card for youngsters, even though they do involve certain problems.

One Ohio library did try a collection of small pets which could be loaned on the same basis as books. It included such creatures as turtles, guppies, finches, parakeets, canaries, hamsters, gerbils, white mice, tropical fish, salamanders and guinea pigs. These were donated by two pet shops after a lone turtle walked into the library one day and decided to stay. Children begged to borrow him and thus the idea for the pet-loaning collection began.

Fritz Stein, who was then librarian of the Garfield Heights Library, says that the collection was eventually phased out, the pets distributed to pet shops, a children's zoo, and numerous private families in the area. During wide publicity about the collection, he received about sixty inquiries from other libraries as to how to set up a pet library and several later reported they had done so with success. He cautions, "I would only recommend that other libraries use a pet collection if they take proper precautions." Proper precautions at his library included close cooperation with the Humane Society and the Cleveland Animal Protective League, with a veterinarian and several biology teachers. The children checking out pets received a booklet on proper care and the necessary food for the two-week loan period.

Other libraries have had pet displays for special occasions. A Cape Cod library discovered how to please its young patrons without turning the library into a year-round animal preserve. During National Library Week they invited the curator of the local Museum of Natural History to come and talk about "books and the natural history of Cape Cod." He brought a live raccoon that performed for the delighted children. There was also considerable excitement when several harmless live snakes were passed around among the young audience. Handling snakes was great fun for the small fry, but I wonder if afterwards librarians reached for books a bit more gingerly, just in case a reptile remained behind?

Then again maybe not, for equanimity upon encountering all sorts of living creatures is an essential quality for librarians — especially Children's Librarians. Many are the toads, small green snakes, and assorted insects that have been thrust under my nose, always with the avowed purpose of needing identification. I have a strong suspicion, however, that under such conditions a librarian is being tested to see if she shudders or squeals. If she does, she will be classified as "the kind you can tease"; if she doesn't, "the kind you can talk to."

Bringers of reptilian wildlife are generally male, but it was a teen-age California girl who asked for material on lizards. When the librarian hesitated momentarily, the girl added, "This kind," and pulled a small green lizard attached to a string from under the collar of her jacket.

Although not precisely an animal story, another incident also involves lizards. A very small patron tiptoed up to the librarian's desk in an Iowa library.

"Please, I want the book about the lizard," she requested.

"What lizard?" queried the librarian.

"Oh, you know. 'We're off to see the lizard, the wonderful lizard of Oz.' "

This young lady had evidently been watching the old Judy Garland movie on television.

Two pet goldfish created wide interest at a branch of the Vancouver Public Library. The honor of cleaning the fish bowl went to certain of the children. The fish rode out from the librarian's desk to the kitchen in stately style on top of one of the book trucks. A child, watching this performance one day, asked where the fish were going. The librarian explained that they were going to be cleaned.

"Oh," said the little girl, enlightened, "you mean to be cut up, like when my Daddy catches fish he cleans them too."

Among non-human visitors reported by an Ohio library were a hamster (who escaped from his owner's pocket and had to be rounded up), a chameleon (he was equipped with a collar and chain), and a Seeing Eye dog who brought his mistress to a Branch library for a talk and thus stimulated the circulation of books on dogs.

It's been my experience, though, that books on dogs — or indeed any kind of animal — scarcely need pushing. They are by far the most popular category with young patrons, excepting, perhaps, mysteries.

Speaking of dogs, from the number of times items appear in newspapers on the subject "Dog Bites Book", it seems a lot of dogs are in the doghouse for being too rough on books. Typical of such universal canine episodes are these:

Wichita, Kansas (Associated Press): "The City Library reports that certain of its books on dog care and training are getting dog-eared. Some of the books bear definite evidence of having been chewed on by household pets."

Mexborough, England (United Press International): "A book well chewed by a dog has been returned to the public library. Its title: 'Scientific Dog Breeding and Management.' "

In addition to these shaggy stories in the press, I have personally viewed quite a few bitten books which subsequently had to be rebound or replaced at the borrower's expense.

Despite this dog-ged desire to literally chew up the rules, most animal owners seem optimistic about raising their pets to be well-groomed, loyal, and obedient. One such patron, mindful of the famous Dr. Spock's books about babies, requested "a kind of Dr. Spock book" for puppies.

Then there was the little boy who, returning his books to a Missouri library, thrust a brown paper bag at the astonished assistant and commanded, "Here, hold this while I pick out my books." The library assistant found herself holding the sack — with a tiny puppy inside.

When a librarian saw a little girl bringing her apprehensive-looking Siamese cat into the children's section where a little boy had his cocker spaniel on a leash, she hastily pointed out that it wasn't a good idea to mix cats and dogs in a library.

"Oh, that's all right," said the boy reassuringly, "We won't let them get *married*."

A creepy cat story comes from a library in Hawaii. One day a staff member came in a back door and observed that there was a dead cat in the trash barrel. Immediately other members of the staff remembered that for quite a while they had been smelling an odd odor.

One look in the trash barrel verified the news for there, glassy-eyed, stiff, and stark, was a cat looking definitely deceased.

The city department in charge of removing dead animals was called and remarkably soon two men and a large truck arrived. Voices were heard muttering outside, and then one of the men came in and inquired in puzzled tones, "Where's the cat?"

With averted head and dramatic finger, one of the librarian's pointed to the barrel.

"No cat inside the barrel," insisted the man.

Just then the other man nudged his companion and pointed to a spot well beneath the truck. There sat puss briskly licking his fur. Then, with a sophisticated leer, he stood up, stretched, and majestically stalked off, no doubt to begin the enjoyment of his remaining eight lives.

The men took off in their truck in a great huff, and the librarian retired to her desk to ponder the curious case of the cataleptic cat.

On one of those prematurely warm days in spring, when you simply have to open the library door and let in the fragrant, drowsy warmth, it's not unusual to have cats or dogs wander in on their own. Dogs may dash about in eager exploration, upset-ting waste baskets and setting book trucks to rolling, while cats sneak quietly by, so that you first see them as a shadow out of the corner of your eye.

As to which is more literary-minded, that is open to ques-tion. But there is at least one instance in which a cat appeared to be a creature of culture. Sitting on a little girl's lap, he enjoyed following her finger as she scanned the words on the printed page. Left to right, left to right, went his head just as though he, too, were reading.

Like the patron who wanted "a kind of Dr. Spock book" to tell him how to bring up his dog, many people ask for informa-tion as to the best way to breed, feed, and heal animals of their ills. "How long before my hamster will have babies?" "How many worms will I have to feed this baby robin that fell out of its nest?"are typical questions of concern.

A young boy who acquired a pigeon as a pet came into his library to ask about books on pigeon diseases. After being shown one which discussed pigeons and their care, he still had a problem. His pigeon's symptom — "His eyes seem to be pop-ping out" — wasn't mentioned. When informed there were no other books on this subject, he apparently gave up on the pigeon for his next question was, "Do you have one on dissect-ing birds?"

Popular as are books about dogs, cats, and assorted wild animals, horses inspire the most devoted group of young read-ers — usually girls from about 8 to 14. These children often go through a period when they politely but firmly refuse to read about any other subject. They don't quite trust the librarian when she says they have read every book the library owns on horses, and she will find them searching the card catalog just to make sure they have not skipped a title with "horse," "pony," "stallion," or "mare" in it.

It is understandable that skilled young horsewomen are eager to read every volume about horses. But by no means do all little girls who devour horse stories own a horse or even ride one. I often ask children taking out books on horses this ques-tion and there is a certain wistfulness to many of the replies:

"I don't believe my parents will ever buy me a horse, but at least I can read about them." Or —

"I did ride a horse once." Then, candidly, "It was really a little pony."

Owning, loving, and caring for live pets is an incentive for reading animal stories, of course. But the affinity felt by most children for all non-human creatures goes beyond that. They consider animals wonderful subjects to read about be they real or imaginary. To wit, these whimsical queries:

Small Boy: "Do you have any books on how to raise pets?"

Librarian: "Certainly. What kind of pets?"

Small boy: "Dinosaurs."

(Dinosaur books — of which there have been a good number during the past two decades — are popular with children who are younger than the horse-loving set. Boys and girls of about 6 to 10 delight in tales of these extinct reptiles.)

Young patron: "I want a book on how to tame wild animals."

Librarian: "What kind of wild animals?"

Young patron: "Turtles."

Patrons with tails accompany their owners to libraries only occasionally, but are never far from young minds and hearts. Because of this, animal stories will continue to loom large in children's literature.

Chapter Four

Teen Tales

Today's teen-agers receive a disproportionate amount of publicity. The news media often spotlights them in rebellious roles: as rioters, dissenters, drug addicts, hippies. At other times they are bathed in the warm glow of adult approval and depicted as serious, intelligent, high-minded, and idealistic. Actually, as with any age group, teen-agers are individuals who differ in make-up. Most are neither saint nor sinner. However, the combination of youthful intensity — always characteristic of adolescents — and the accelerating ferment of social change does often cause them to act in such ways as to draw attention to themselves. That is why teen-agers have been increasingly analyzed until, as a group, they have become overly self-conscious about playing a "role" in society. Still, young people do have, today as always, real and special needs and problems. It is a legitimate aim for responsible adults to try to help them find some of the answers for themselves.

Those librarians who work with teen-agers, whether in special Young Adult Departments or in generalized collections, can contribute to this process, not only by matching books to patrons, but by awakening new interests, and generally being the sort of persons in whom young people like to confide.

Children's Rooms were opened in libraries as long ago as the 1890's, and today even libraries with a very limited staff usually employ a Children's Librarian. In contrast, only larger libraries, as a rule, have Young Adult Departments with a specially trained librarian in charge, although more are adding this service each year. Many libraries do provide a few shelves, an alcove, or a room containing books of a type to appeal to older junior readers.

The Cleveland, Ohio, Public Library pioneered in service to young adults when it opened its Robert Louis Stevenson Room in 1925. Another innovation occurred when the New York Public

Library, in 1941, opened the Donnell Library Center with its Nathan Straus Young Adult Library. The latter was designed to serve readers of from 13 to 21 years of age. Other libraries with Young Adult Departments indicate that their borrowers range from 14 to 18 (Boston Public Library) or from 12 to 20.

Though they may differ slightly as to what ages are served, Young Adult Librarians agree as to why such collections came into being. In years past, young people who outgrew the Children's Room often stopped coming to the library. When the time arrived for them to graduate to adult collections, they were frequently bewildered by new authors and by subject matter which was boring or beyond their comprehension. Hence, except for an occasional volume taken for school assignments, they often ceased to be borrowers. As adults, many did not resume recreational reading. Recognition of this state of affairs by librarians, plus two developments — young people who were increasingly educated to have more lively, diversified interests; and publication of books of greater suitability and scope for this age group — made special services for young adults both possible and inevitable.

Though some children cannot wait to cross the bridge from childhood to adolescence, others are reluctant to do so. One boy, about 12 years old, asked his librarian for material for a speech he had to give on "why these adults are always trying to push us children into adultery." After gulping down a giggle, the librarian showed him where to look for information on the various aspects of the early maturation of teen-agers.

Collections which serve such a wide age range have to include books on many reading levels. Some are duplicates of titles in the Children's Department. Youngsters of 12 to 15 may still prefer these, but turn up their noses at "baby books" if directed to the Children's Room.

In the last couple of decades a new form of literature has emerged: the teen-age novel. Some of these are written with real skill and a genuine understanding of the problems encountered by adolescents groping toward adulthood. They are popular with young people — especially girls.

Also included are familiar classics, and many current titles on an adult level, both fiction and non-fiction.

Young Adult Librarians spend a good deal of time and thought in evaluating books and compiling reading lists; the results are anything but dull. For example, Boston Public Library came up with such punchy, provocative titles for lists as: "Don't Go Near the Water — Unless You Read a Book" (skin and scuba diving, water sports, boating, etc.); "Haunted Heroines: Haunted Houses" (from *Jane Eyre* to *Mistress of Mellyn*); and "Books and Looks" (good grooming, fiction about plain and pretty girls).

Female teen-agers are preoccupied with personal appearance; at home they spend nearly as much time peering into a mirror as talking on the telephone. Even today's casual blue jeans look has to be properly put together. In the library girls are avid readers of such magazines as *Seventeen* and *Mademoiselle*. And they are always on the alert for new fads.

One young lady, evidently interested in creative styling, asked a librarian, "Do you have a picture of Julius Caesar so that I can model my hairdo after his?"

Much of her concern about personal appearance springs, quite naturally, from a girl's desire to appeal to boys. In reading, preoccupation with love and dating is apparent by the 13- to 17-year-old's preference for romances written especially for her. Heroines of these young-adult romances are usually older than the reader — ranging from the late high school period through college and early career to young marriage — yet they always must be someone with whom she can identify. Now that "someone" is changing. When I queried librarians about five years ago as to a representative romantic story popular with girls, several mentioned the fictionalized biography about Elizabeth Barrett and Robert Browning, *How Do I Love Thee?* Today it would probably be a title such as Zindel's *I Never Loved Your Mind* — quite possibly in paperback.

The boy-girl relationship, its potentialities and problems, is a subject with which every library deals. Sometimes it does so in serious ways: with carefully selected books on adolescence, dating, and sex. At other times, the subject has its amusing facets.

One library received this reference question by telephone: "I am writing a thesis on the art of kissing. Could you tell me some techniques?"

A parent had this puzzler: "An older boy comes uninvited and unwanted to see my 12-year-old daughter. Do you have a book telling me how to send him home without making him mad at me?"

A West coast library found in a card catalog drawer, filed under "Boys", a card which read: "If you want a date — call me." His name and phone number were given.

Librarians agree that today's young people are more knowledgeable about many things than were their parents at the same age. They are keenly interested in scientific subjects such as space exploration; they want books about various careers; and they feel strongly about the problems of integration, world understanding, and peace. Intelligent and curious, they present both a joy and a challenge.

Another sort of challenge is the slow reader, or almost non-reader, who somehow finds his way to the library. When a librarian can patiently and skillfully guide him to the point where he discovers that reading can be a pleasure, she knows real satisfaction. With such an aim in view, Boston Public Library made up one book list and headed it "Books for Young People Who Still Hate Books." They did not say how effective it was in helping achieve the desired purpose!

Every library has to cope with reluctant borrowers. Their dislike for reading is expressed in various ways.

"I want a narrow book for a book report," one boy requested. "I only have 'til Monday to read it."

Another youngster asked, "Do you have any books arranged by the number of pages in the book?"

A high-school student was overheard complaining that he could not find a *short* three-act play. His companion suggested he take out a one-act play.

"Oh, no," he protested. "That way, I'd never know how it came out!"

One method of attracting new readers is to show motion picture films. These are not chosen solely for the reluctant reader, of course. They must be stimulating to many young people. But more than one librarian reports that a non-reader, intrigued by an advertised film, has come to view it, discovered a book to his liking, and become a regular reader.

Numerous other activities are offered in Young Adult Departments. There are exhibits of various handicrafts; demonstrations of such physical feats as weight-lifting and karate; planned group discussions on topical subjects. As one librarian remarked: "Everything from urban renewal to judo interests our teen-agers."

Whatever the activity, whether it be teen-age poets reading their own work, young artists taking part in exhibits, or adolescents questioning an adult lecturer, participation by young patrons themselves is the key to success. Ideally, the Young Adult section, with its colorful, comfortable surroundings, its informal atmosphere, and friendly librarians makes the young person feel this is *his* or *her* library — a good place to come.

Being fallible, some librarians and patrons do not fit this ideal picture. Certain librarians — usually not those trained to work with young people — belong to the old school which still holds that children of any age should be seen, not heard. Certain teen-agers are rowdy and rebellious. When these two types clash, there are apt to be fireworks.

A mild example of this was the boy who, disgusted at being asked to make out a second application card after he'd lost his first, grumbled: "You're passin' too many laws!"

Then there are those teen-agers who insist on smoking in libraries even though they know it is forbidden. In one instance, a librarian observed a high-school student, cigarette in mouth, and tapped him on the shoulder. "No smoking," she warned.

A few minutes after he'd left, smoke was seen coming out of the mouth of a bronze horse statue on the window sill. Upon investigation, a lighted cigarette was found in the horse's mouth.

Young guys and gals delight in thinking up snappy comebacks. During the Chubby Checker craze some years ago, a teen-ager asked a librarian, "Can Oliver Twist?"

In a California library an adult patron remarked to a librarian, "You seem to be out of Spinoza today."

A student standing near the desk was overheard muttering, sotto voce, "Why not try the pastrami at the corner stand?"

As for protests, this may take the prize. A teen-age boy vehemently insisted that he ought not to be charged any fine on his overdue book. The assistant on duty explained, emphatically, that he must pay a fine because the book was returned late.

"But it did me no good," he protested.

"What do you mean?" asked the assistant.

"Well, you see," he explained, "this book is about learning to ride horseback. I read it, went out horseback riding and look what happened."

He removed his coat to show an arm in a cast and sling.

"I fell off, broke my arm, and that's why I shouldn't have to pay the fine. The book did me no good."

Evidently this youngster thought the library's motto should be "Satisfaction guaranteed or your money back."

The attitude of some defiant teen-agers is summed up in this piece, entitled HAPPINESS, which was written by a student and left surreptitiously in a New England library. Not one to be easily daunted, the librarian prepared an ANSWER and posted both on the bulletin board.

HAPPINESS

"HAPPINESS is going to the library and not having parents ask
    you a lot of questions about why you are going.
HAPPINESS is being able to come to the library and speaking to
    some friends without the librarians yelling at you.
HAPPINESS would be not having any librarians to tell us they'll
    call the police if we don't state our names! (I SCARED!) (sic)
HAPPINESS is having no librarian!!"

48

ANSWER

"Youth is an age of insecurity, restlessness, inconsistency and indecision according to Pat Boone in his book *'Twixt Twelve and Twenty*. The library is a perfect place to meet the girl friend; a means of getting away from the parents in order to have a good time for a few hours; and a good way of getting out of studying, the excuse — of course — 'I must go to the library.'

"When we get there, the librarian yells at you — you haven't done anything except talk. Why the restrictions? Adults should be allowed a place in the library where they can be quiet. The library is a place for children, youth, and adults. Not *just* youth.

"If youth cannot obey the rules of consideration for others and disturbs the peace, then according to the laws of the land, force can be used. If there were no librarians, who would help you with your reference problems; who would get your magazines for you and who would find the books you need and can't find?

"Why does youth rebel to discipline? Because they are trying to assert themselves and grow up. I know, believe it or not. Your librarian was once a youth and went through the same growing pains."

Three observations may be made on this dialogue between teen-ager and librarian.

First: Malcontents such as these do lounge around libraries, generally cluttering up the place, but they are in a minority.

Second: When more libraries set aside a special room or department for young adults, there will be less incidents of an unpleasant nature. Now, as this librarian indicated, teen-agers must often share quarters with children or adults and this means too many restrictions are necessary — making for a punitive rather than a pleasant atmosphere.

Third: Praiseworthy as it is for a librarian to recall her own youth and be properly sympathetic, this is not enough. Time has a way of blurring memories until we remember ourselves as more perfect than we were. It is a natural failing of adults to say — or at least to think — in a somewhat self-righteous way, "Now, when I was your age . . . " In addition to feeling sympathy, librarians should be trained in adolescent psychology and be familiar with youthful tastes and goals.

Expressions change from generation to generation. In an account of the opening of a Children's Room which took place in the early 1900's one boy was quoted as saying, "Golly, this is great." A number of years ago, when I worked in a recently opened Children's Room, several youngsters came up with, "Gee, this is neat." Today, I expect, a similar occasion would be greeted with, "Man, it's cool."

The emotions are the same: the language different. The truly hip librarian who works with young people understands both.

Chapter Five

Topsy-Turvy Titles

Some years ago the late Dr. Sigmund Spaeth appeared on stage and radio in a musical act in which he ferreted out classic themes which had been plagiarized and turned into popular tunes. These demonstrations earned him the title of "tune detective."

While being a "tune detective" was a somewhat specialized occupation, being a "title detective" is the daily duty of many a librarian. Indeed, one wonders if L.S. *really* stands for a degree in Library Science or in Literary Sleuthing. It's a pity library schools do not include compulsory courses in reading patrons' sub-conscious minds. If they did, requests like this might pose fewer problems.

"I read a book about 20 years ago about a man who lived his life over again. I can't remember the author's name or the name of the book, but I know it was yellow and was right in this section."

The amazing thing is that most of the time, even without a Literary Sleuthing degree, librarians do find the books patrons have in mind. All the following topsy-turvy titles were righted by clever title detecting on the part of librarians.

Requested: Who is Your School Master?
Book wanted: *Hoosier Schoolmaster*

Requested: Entombed with an Infant
Book wanted: *In Tune with the Infinite*

Requested: Lady Godiva's Friends
Book wanted: *Lady Chatterley's Lover*

Requested: My Heart is Wounded, They Buried My Knee
Book wanted: *Bury My Heart at Wounded Knee*

Requested: From Here to Maternity
Book wanted: *From Here to Eternity*

Requested: The Missing Hand
Book wanted: *Farewell to Arms*

Requested: Head of the Family
Book wanted: *The Godfather*

Requested: The Return of Maggie O'Toole
Book wanted: *The Search for Bridey Murphy*

Some titles cause more confusion than others. For instance, several librarians reported requests for the equally elusive title and creature, the *Abominable Snowman*. Those seeking this book asked for "At the Bottom of the Snowman" and "Abdominal Snowman."

Another title which caused multiple trouble was *Lord of the Flies*. All patrons were sure of was that it had entomological connotations. A Colorado patron asked for "King of the Bees" and a Florida reader wanted "King of the Ants."

In more than one instance the teen-ager's favorite, *Catcher in the Rye*, was requested by boys under the title "Catch Her in the Rye." Could be girls and the song "Comin' Through the Rye" got mixed up in their minds!

"Gin a body meet a body,
Comin' through the rye
Gin a body kiss a body,
Need a body cry?"

Children's librarians are especially adept at untwisting tangled titles. Here are some misnamed books requested by small tots — or their parents.

Requested: Daddy's Dinosaur
Book wanted: *My Father's Dragon*

Requested: The Green-nosed Kitty
Book wanted: *Blue-Eyed Pussy*

Requested: The Wooden Kid
Book wanted: *Pinocchio*

Requested: Winnie the Pooch
Book wanted: *Winnie-the-Pooh*

Requested: Three Story Animals
Book wanted: *Prehistoric Animals*

Requested: Harry the Dirty Book
Book wanted: *Harry the Dirty Dog*

Older children also have title troubles such as these.

Requested: Allergy in a Country Churchyard
Book wanted: *Elegy Written in a Country Churchyard*

Requested: St. Francis the Sissy
Book wanted: *St. Francis of Assisi*

Requested: Five Pennies and the Sun
Book wanted: *The Moon and Sixpence*

Young minds appear to run in certain channels, judging by the muddled titles they dredge up. Predictably, one is gastronomic. A youngster asking for "Banana Royal" really wanted *Banners Royal*. Another hungry patron requested "Chow Mein and His Knights" but settled for *Charlemagne and His Knights*.

Topical names and subject matter also weave their way into wrongly-remembered titles. A few years back more than one request was received for "Robinson Khrushchev" (*Robinson Crusoe*). "Jacqueline Hyde" (*Dr. Jekyll and Mr. Hyde*) was also in demand.

Local origin can also get entwined in a title. A librarian at the Bangor, Maine, Public Library was baffled by a request for "Lives of the Bangor Dancers." Upon further questioning, it developed that the patron wanted *Lives of the Bengal Lancers*.

Some students appear to wage a losing struggle with titles of classics. To wit:

Requested: Warren Pease
Book wanted: *War and Peace*

Requested: Homeless Idiot
Book wanted: Homer's *Iliad*

Requested: The Oddities
Book wanted: Homer's *Odyssey*

Requested: The Merchant of Venus
Book wanted: *The Merchant of Venice*

Requested: A book on "coyotes"
Book wanted: *Don Quixote*

If one thing is clear about mixed-up titles, it is that many of them are sound-alikes. Apparently syllable sounds stick in the mind of many a patron more firmly than does the sense of the subject matter. Such was the case with a high school girl in a Pennsylvania library. Rather shyly, she asked a librarian for the book "Mature Beauty Care." The librarian, upon checking the card catalog, reported that the library did not have such a book.

"Will any other book on beauty culture do?" she asked.

The girl smiled a bit vaguely. "Well," she admitted, "I guess it only *sounds* like that."

After a fair amount of detective work, it was discovered that she wanted Booth Tarkington's *Monsieur Beaucaire*.

Higher education and responsible position do not rule out boners. A legislator, whose state shall be nameless, kept several members of a library staff busy for hours searching for a book — or the listing of a book — by the title, "The Armored Chinaman." Eventually it developed that the book he actually was seeking was *The Chink in the Armour*.

Then there was the flustered lady who hurried into an Iowa library and demanded "The Rapes of Grath" (*The Grapes of Wrath*).

54

Usually title confusion is caused by sound-alikes or titles not yet conceived by any author. But sometimes patrons ask for one actual title while really wanting another, which makes for a different kind of problem. In a Los Angeles branch library, for instance, a lady asked for *Dinner at Antoine's*. When handed the book by the librarian, the patron realized it was an earlier meal she had in mind — *Breakfast at Tiffany's*!

A most puzzling series of requests for a non-existent title was received by another branch of the Los Angeles Public Library. A patron, evidently feeling he had discovered gold between book covers, generously suggested to his friends that they hustle on down to the library to share his good fortune. One person after another insisted he wanted to borrow "Beer Markets — How to Service and Make Money in Them." After several librarians were nearing the point of collapse, one of them finally deciphered the requests : *Bear Markets – How to Survive and Make Money in Them*.

Sometimes it is the librarians who cause the confusion. One librarian, phoning a patron about a reserved book, announced: *"A World Beyond"* (Ruth Montgomery's description of the afterlife) "is here for you."

A young female librarian phoned a male patron and declared cheerfully: "I now have *Everything You Always Wanted to Know About Sex*."

A mother with an active toddler in tow was hastily leaving the library before the youngster could tear the place apart. But as she passed the charging desk she paused to ask, "Would you reserve Daphne du Maurier's latest book for me?"

The librarian, recalling the book's title, said, *"Don't Look Now."*

"I'm not," replied the startled mother. "I'm going just as soon as I pick up Johnny's cap."

Chapter Six

Reference

If correcting titles calls for some slight sleuthing on the part of the librarian, answering reference questions frequently demands detection in depth. This challenge of finding an elusive bit of information or answering the seemingly impossible question is what makes reference work so fascinating.

The public's confidence in a librarian's ability can also be a pleasant by-product of reference work, but often patrons have an exaggerated idea of her personal store of knowledge. Probably the pet peeve of Reference Librarians are those patrons who phone or come to the desk and say, "Now don't bother to look this up, but do you happen to know . . . "

To the librarian's courteous reply, "Just a moment. I'll check it for you," the patron answers, "Never mind," slams down the receiver, or dashes out the library door.

Would that such persons might ponder the words of author Samuel Johnson: "Knowledge is of two kinds: we know a subject ourselves, or we know where we can find information upon it."

The more of the first kind of knowledge a librarian has the better, of course. After all, if you know just where the Easter eggs are hidden you get to them faster than if you have to search in all directions. The more quickly a correct answer is found, the more time there is for doing other reference work. And, too, the public is often impatient.

But the really essential tool is the second kind of knowledge. Here there is no personal limitation of remembered facts. The only limitations are the total resources of a library. For reference questions may be answered, not just from a separate group of books marked "reference", but from any book, periodical, pamphlet, or special information file owned by that particular library.

There is danger in answering reference questions from personal knowledge alone. An off-the-cuff answer, given in certainty, can prove embarrassing when you later discover you were wrong and the patron is long gone, with name and address unknown!

A directive from the Chief Librarian in one library where I worked was, "Don't answer any reference question without confirming it, even if the patron only wants to know how to spell CAT."

Although this was a humorous overstatement to make a point, I generally followed his advice. However, one day a patron phoned in to ask how to spell *Rockefeller* in *Rockefeller Center*, New York City. As I finished spelling it, without book in hand, the Head of the Reference Department entered our office. Hanging up the telephone, I faced her and declared a bit defensively, "Well, I *do* know how to spell Rockefeller."

Cooly, with only a hint of a smile, she queried, "They're relatives of yours?"

Another aspect of reference work which makes it so interesting is the infinite variety of questions asked. They range from practical to philosophical, from trivial to scholarly, from the ridiculous to the sublime. One request follows another with utter unpredictability. Work on a bibliography for the Representative of a Congressional District is interrupted by a 15-year-old boy who stammers that he needs "something to tell me about dating." Before his request can be filled, the phone rings. A frantic mother wants descriptions of the poisonous coral snake and the non-poisonous scarlet snake — or false coral snake — which look much alike. She's not sure which one she just saw in her yard. And so it goes.

The larger the library, the more people served, the greater the scope of reference services offered. Small and medium-sized libraries are less likely than the large library to have a full-fledged reference service in the form of a separately staffed department. But no library, however modest in size, completely escapes the reference-type question.

Reference questions fall into certain categories. Some of the simplest have to do with the location of books in the library. Many of these could be answered by any staff member, but often the patron thinks this kind of query is a reference question and comes for assistance. And sometimes the question is so puzzling it is referred to the Reference Department by another librarian, as was this one.

"Do you have a red book on controversial subjects?"

Then there are directional or informational questions about the community: "Where is a good place to eat?" "Do you know when the Museum opens?" "What is the oldest building in the city?"

When the locale of a library is famous in history or legend, informational questions can be an almost daily occurrence. For instance, at Dodge City, Kansas (portrayed in TV Westerns), the librarian reports that "sometimes it is difficult to convince the tourists who stop in to do a little research that Matt Dillon is pure fiction. After all, in *Gunsmoke* he seems as real as Wyatt Earp."

Information about noted citizens with local ties is also in demand. The library in Hyannis, Massachusetts, receives many questions, pertinent and impertinent, about the famous Kennedy clan. And Mrs. Dwight D. Eisenhower was of interest to a Colorado neighbor. (Mrs. Eisenhower's parents lived in Denver.) "Where," asked this patron, "would you find the address of Mamie Eisenhower's grocery store in Gettysburg?" The gentleman was told that so far as the Colorado Springs Library knew the former First Lady was not engaged in business — grocery or otherwise.

City directories are well-thumbed volumes in many libraries. Information sought is usually found with little difficulty by patrons, but one young lady phoned the Reference Department of her library for help. "Could you," she asked, "check the City Directory and see if my boy friend got married last year?"

Another reference worker was asked the location of a small town in the Texas Panhandle. After being given this information, the patron wanted to know every turn of the road thereabouts because he was planning to fly there using the roads as direction guides.

Questions concerning population figures are usually uncomplicated and not especially humorous, but one librarian had to chuckle when a young lad called the Reference Department and asked for the population of the United States. "Please, ma'am, go slow," he begged. "I'm only 11 years old."

Reference questions can be divided into two general types — "ready reference" and "research". "Ready reference" questions can be answered in a matter of minutes, often from standard reference works on or near the librarian's desk. "Research" questions require more time and skill on the librarian's part because they are unusual, involved, or otherwise difficult.

Questions that at first appear to be simple may turn out to be not so "ready" after all. Even those having to do with spelling and definitions of words often demand much more than an automatic response from the librarian. Sometimes such questions take her breath away and leave her with no response at all!

A man phoned a library and spelled a very odd-sounding word. The librarian looked in an unabridged dictionary but failed to find it. Again she checked with the patron and the dictionary. Still no luck.

"I'm sorry," she reported, "but I do not find the word. Would you mind telling me where you saw it?"

His cheerful reply: "Oh, in no special place, ma'am. I just dreamed it last night and wondered what it meant."

Something more than dictionary definition was required from the librarian who was tossed this one over the telephone.

"I can't find female trouble in the dictionary," a worried woman complained. "What is it?" After being given a brief explanation she asked, "And do men have it?"

A male patron phoned to ask for the definition of *Homo sapien.* Upon being told that it was "Man, regarded as a biological species," he whistled. "Whew, I called a fellow that the other day and he nearly hit me!"

60

Another man phoned to say, "I have a letter here from my boss and he says I've been terminated. What does that mean?"

The caller was given a couple of dictionary definitions, but as he still sounded confused, the librarian was finally forced to explain frankly, "What that means, Sir, is that you have been fired."

As she hung up, the librarian couldn't help chuckling. But then she suddenly sobered to the significance of a man who was unfamiliar with a fairly common word but somehow knew that the Library was the place to call for help.

Other frequent SOSes concern etiquette. A fair example is the telephone request I received my first day as a Reference Assistant. The patron, puzzled by a notation on an invitation, wanted to know the meaning of R.S.V.P. Upon being told that *Répondez, s'il vous plaît* meant that a reply was requested, she then demanded the proper French pronunciation.

On a similar subject, a library was queried as to where to start writing on note paper used for thank-you notes. Two librarians consulted Emily Post, Amy Vanderbilt — and each other. Then they quizzed the patron as to whether or not the paper was monogrammed. By folding a piece of paper at their end of the telephone line, they came up with a satisfactory answer.

Reference Librarians are asked for counsel on matters stretching from the cradle to the grave. Surely some of the most moving etiquette questions come from the recently bereaved. Distressed widows seek advice on proper clothing to be worn at the funeral and on fitting replies to letters of condolence.

Other patrons ask what gifts are correct for a special wedding anniversary or a christening and what the duties of godparents are.

Although not a matter of etiquette, scarcely a day goes by that some expectant mother does not request help in deciding "what to name the baby." Often the not-so-obviously pregnant woman or the father appears embarrassed and gets to this question by degrees.

One big, shy young man asked for something on the history of names. Shown books on heraldry, he shook his head. Finally, he stammered that what he really needed was a book that would list a baby's name meaning "unexpected".

Domestic dilemmas and decisions prompt certain questions. If the comparative merits of different makes of household appliances, such as dishwashers and vacuum cleaners, are wanted, the patron is referred to consumer magazines or pamphlets.

When it comes to cooking, finding recipes for special dishes can be frustrating. In one case, the entire library staff pitched in to aid a German bride who was homesick for some home cooked sauerkraut. She was tired of the stuff she bought at the store and wanted to make her own. Though this particular library had a large cookbook section, no recipes for sauerkraut could be found for some time. Then a book's index did list it. Eagerly turning to the page, the German girl read: "Open can, heat and serve."

Ready reference questions include many requests for sports scores, records, and champions, usually easily available. Sometimes, though, more detailed information about a sport or game is desired. Then all possible sources are used to supply it, not excluding eavesdroppers!

A question about chess came to one library by telephone. If the pawn was moved to the king's line could thus and so be done? The man couldn't find this described in any of the rules books he owned. As the librarian was explaining that since she didn't play chess, she, too, would have to use books to try to find the answer, a man walked up to the desk and stood listening to her conversation. At this point she was repeating the problem back to the patron on the phone. The bystander interrupted, "Yes, yes, you can do that," so she let the two talk to each other, and they had a brief, neat conversation about the value of the pawn at the king's line.

Quite a lot of questions come from businessmen and secretaries. Indeed a few libraries, such as the Free Library of Philadelphia, operate a special business branch. But mostly such services are provided by reference or business departments in the central libraries.

By no means are all such queries ponderous in nature. This one left the librarian asking some questions herself. A sweet young thing came up to her desk and inquired innocently, "Do you have a book that tells what to do when you go on a trip with your boss?"

Answers to another type of "ready reference" question, that sought by club officers on parliamentary procedure, can be quickly found in such books as *Robert's Rules of Order*. But when club members or city officials need help in gathering material for speeches, reference in depth may be required.

Election times can be particularly hectic. I recall that during the 1952 Presidential Campaign the Head of our department was busy typing up a bibliography on Dwight D. Eisenhower while I tracked down material on Adlai E. Stevenson. Librarians supposedly being nonpartisan while on duty, we flipped a coin for our assignments.

Volumes such as *Who's Who in America* and *Celebrity Register* are among the most used in the library, for the average person's curiosity about his fellow human beings — especially those more noted than he — is nearly unquenchable. Such information is usually easy to find, but some questions, or patrons, give the librarian a hard time.

One elderly gentleman called to ask for Jean Harlow's phone number. Nothing the librarian said could convince him that she was no longer living. "After all," he insisted, "I saw her just last week on The Late, Late Show."

Then there are seekers after the family tree. No more determined, single-minded patron exists than the one who comes to ferret out his honorable ancestors. Some large libraries have special departments or librarians to deal with genealogical research, but for the most part this falls to the lot of the Reference Librarian. She usually contents herself with indicating the relevant collection and leaves the amateur genealogist to do his own research, for tracing an entire family history can be a time-consuming process.

This fact was evidently overlooked by a Junior High School student. "I'm supposed to look up my family tree back to the time my ancestors came to America," he announced cheerfully. "The name is Smith."

Asked the librarian, "When is this assignment due?"

"Tomorrow."

Another student's request: "Please, do you have a book that would give the family tree of the Greek Gods?"

And then there was the time I received a letter from out-of-state requesting that somebody at the library go to a certain cemetery and "look around" to see if the correspondent's distant relatives were buried there. Much as I might have liked to spend my free day searching a graveyard for the lady's ancestors, this was quite impossible as the cemetery she mentioned was not even in our city.

Questions which come by mail can often be answered more satisfactorily than this one, but it's only fair to say that librarians do not look with any great joy on the reference question by mail. Some queries are intelligent and intelligible, but too many times the patron does not know how to express himself and the result is confusion. For instance, a Southern library received a letter asking for information on "how to preserve a mule with a fence around it."

Reference Departments being the busy places they are, with question following question in quick succession, it is not wise to enter into a protracted correspondence to clear up a cloudy point. Many libraries, however, do answer such mail courteously but briefly.

Telephoned questions are another matter. In my experience, nearly half of all reference questions are phoned in. Of course, this is not so true of small town libraries where far fewer calls of this type are received.

Such over-the-wire queries are varied in nature. Some concern consumer purchases. That public libraries serve all strata of society and not just the citizen of modest means was evident when a lady called to ask our help in deciding between a mink or ermine jacket. What did the fashion magazines say was "in" this season? (One jacket the caller was considering was priced at $2,050 and this was quite a few years back!)

While medical and legal advice is often sought over the phone, most libraries limit answers on these subjects to definitions or brief quotable facts. It is not feasible — or ethical — to interpret such complex matters for patrons. After all, few public librarians hold a second degree in law or medicine. However, when it is evident that a patron is desperately in need of professional help, any librarian worth her salt refers them to an appropriate individual or agency. Libraries usually have listings of local legal aid societies, which give assistance free or for a small fee, and community clinics and family counseling services.

Though librarians limit replies to medical questions, they still do come in and often cause a chuckle.

Asked one lady: "Please find me a book on congenial heart diseases."

And another: "Under what sign of the Zodiac do you wean babies?"

As for legal affairs, the greatest number of inquiries have to do with marriage and divorce laws. Often patrons appear impatient for such information, but the record for hasty requests was probably this one.

When a young woman phoned to ask in which state she could be married without a wait, the librarian said she would check to see.

"Please hurry," the young lady urged. "I'm at a pay station and my boy friend is outside double parked with the motor running."

Another telephoned question concerning young love came to a California library. The gentleman calling asked for the meaning of tiger lily in the language of flowers. When told that it was not included in the available lists, he informed the librarian that he understood it meant "Dare to love me?" and asked that it be added to the library's list. "You see," he explained, "I'm sending a tiger lily to my dream girl and am enclosing your library telephone number. Please tell everyone there who answers the phone so she'll be sure to get the message."

One advantage of phoning in a question rather than mailing it is immediacy. Instructions can cope with a problem as the patron seeks to solve it. Sometimes, though, this doesn't work out as planned.

A woman telephoned a Reference Department to ask which way a tree that was being chopped down was likely to fall. While the library assistant was explaining it to her, she suddenly said: "Never mind, it just fell. And it fell the wrong way and landed on a fence!"

Nearly every Saturday morning one woman, evidently without a cookbook to her name, used to call me and ask that I look up a recipe. As cookbooks were not in the reference collection, it took a little time to locate each desired recipe. Once, as I picked up the phone, the lady exclaimed, "Hold everything! Something is burning!" For long minutes, as I awaited her return, the only sound was that of an apparently scorched pan being vigorously scraped. All this while a patron-in-person awaited assistance outside the reference office. This, it might be noted, is the greatest drawback to the telephoned question. Who takes precedence? The patron before you or the insistently ringing telephone?

Most objectionable of all telephone queries are those contest questions which nearly all libraries have suffered at one time or another. Some libraries, in desperation, refuse to answer such requests. Others do. As soon as it is discovered that the library does answer contest questions, phones ring constantly. For clamor, a library at contest time equals any lively newsroom with bulletin bells clanging.

The nerves of one librarian were not helped by a certain caller, working on a prize puzzle, who asked, "How do you spell *kinnikinnick*?" Then, upon being told, the lady added, "Will you please not tell anyone else how to spell it."

Librarians usually take pride in being able to pigeonhole questions into identifiable groupings. (Not only are librarians orderly creatures, but categorization makes it easier to answer future questions.) However, many requests simply defy definition. Some are quite personal in nature. There was, for instance, the lady who wanted to find the address of a perfume manufacturer in a business directory. Years ago, she explained, she had worn this particular perfume to attract the man who was now her husband. Recently he had begun to wander, and so she desperately needed to know where the perfume could be purchased.

Other requests are just plain peculiar. A man called a library to find out what color burnt bronze was. After three Reference Librarians had practically torn the library apart and finally found the description in a book on mineralogy, the patron was asked if he was working on a research paper.

"No," he replied. "I'm a Prophet and the Bible says 'Prophets shall wear shoes of burnt bronze.' " He was on his way to buy a new pair of shoes and didn't know what color to get.

Then there was the lady who was always stumping her library with odd requests. One day she got off on a tack of studying artistic composition, and started looking in the card catalog for material. Her current interest was the use of stripes, so she came up to the reference desk and asked for "the material on vertical files." (She had seen the notation on a catalog card saying to ask the Reference Librarian for material in the Vertical File and thought it referred to vertical stripes. It, of course, referred to pamphlet material kept in the file.)

One gentleman wanted to know where walrus go to die. He thought he would go there and gather tusks. ("And," added the librarian, "he looked like he would too.")

A man came up to a Reference Librarian and asked for a book on taxidermy. All the material was out and she offered to send to another library on interlibrary loan for some books.

"Oh, lady," he protested, "that would be too late; the moose head is already soft."

When this conversation was related to the Head Librarian, he went into gales of laughter. "It's too good to be true," he chortled. "We thought up the same outlandish possibility for a skit in a Workshop on Library Public Relations held six years ago, but I never thought it would actually happen!"

Some oddities occur more because of the librarian's confusion than the patron's. A new, inexperienced library assistant was scheduled to work alone at the reference desk one day. A lady came in and asked for a book about ants. Feeling very virtuous and knowing, the young librarian dashed to the science shelves, seized a six-pound tome entitled *Principles of Entomology,* and bore it triumphantly to the patron. The lady took the book, sat down, and started to peruse it. After perhaps ten minutes, she came back, book in hand, a puzzled look on her face, and said, "But I want to find out how to get rid of them!"

During the course of a cold winter day, a young Canadian Reference Librarian was asked how to tan skin. She replied helpfully, "Have you tried sitting under a sun lamp, Sir?" (He, it developed, was interested in tanning hides.)

Another Reference Librarian searched her collection for a full fifteen minutes looking for books on lily ponds, whereupon it turned out that what the patron wanted was something on singer Lily Pons. To even things up, later that year another patron asked the same librarian for information on lily ponds — really meaning it this time. Hence his reaction was understandably a blank stare when the librarian slowly and distinctly inquired, "Are you sure, Sir, you do not mean Leely Pons?"

Some questions are really staggering, but they do indicate the amount of faith patrons have that a librarian can come up with an answer to anything. One such question, received by a West Coast library: "Please name all the actresses that appeared on the New York stage between 1900 and 1940."

While it is doubtful that this patron received a complete and exhaustive answer — if he did, the librarian was surely exhausted — some seemingly impossible questions do have accessible answers.

The first reaction of a Washington state librarian to the question, "What is the lowest mountain in the world?" was to throw up her hands in dismay and comment that this came under the heading of "How high is up?" But by searching diligently, she found that there apparently was a fine dividing line between a hill and a mountain. An old *Hill's Manual* listed low as well as high mountains, and the patron was satisfied.

An equally difficult question came to me one time: "Did the Romans eat in a lounging or sitting position?" At first I was amused, but when the standard encyclopedias failed to state what degree of inclination the Romans took during repasts, my own inclination was to doubt that I would find anything. Yet, in time, I discovered in a very old, badly stained, and out of print volume the information that the Romans had, indeed, been said to recline while dining.

What limitations are there on the scope of library reference services? Ideally, very few. As a community information center, the library — particularly its reference division — should unstintingly aid all who quest after knowledge of any sort: students, professional workers, and citizens in every walk of life. Available should be every related service from Readers' Advisory to preparation of bibliographies; from "ready reference" to extensive research. The whole community, not just a segment of it, should be the beneficiary. To this end, a workable motto might be: "When in doubt, double-time it to your library."

In practical terms there are limitations. When short-staffed, as are many libraries because of the lack of professionally trained people, the more complex, time-taking services associated with reference suffer most. Somehow, it is always possible to charge and discharge all the books desired by patrons. And children's services are given priority too. Neighborhood pressures from parents see to that! But, by too many persons, comprehensive reference service is considered a luxury.

Then, proficiency in library science is, in itself, not enough to ensure a really good Reference Librarian. Motivation is also important. Unless a librarian has as great an interest in people as she has in books, she will not be able to fully serve patrons. This is true of any library worker, but especially of the one entrusted with reference problems. Qualities of tact, warmth, and curiosity about her fellow human beings are as essential to her as to a first class social worker. In addition, she has to have a talent for ferreting out obscure bits of information — all of this without losing her emotional balance on the more hectic days.

This — the continual pressure of having too much to do in too little time — is another reason why services performed by Reference Librarians fall short of the ideal. My Reference boss used to say she sometimes thought the only way to proceed efficiently would be to have patrons phone ahead to make appointments with us, so long was the waiting line on our busier days.

With such constant demands on their time and facilities, it is understandable why some librarians hesitate to promote their reference services. Yet, failure to publicize them limits the ideal of service to all. Many times, people I've met on the outside have been astonished to learn of the nuggets of information which could be theirs simply by picking up the phone and calling their local library.

Once hooked, however, patrons will take no substitute for individualized help from a Reference Department. In one library where I worked as Reference Assistant, we were so short-staffed at night that I also filled in at the circulation desk — leaving the reference office unmanned (unwomaned?).

Patrons had been so well indoctrinated by promotion about services available through the Reference Department that when I answered one of the phones at the main desk they would request, "Please connect me with the Reference Department."

If I replied, "May I help you?" they would insist, "No, I want the Reference Department."

Sometimes this dialogue was varied by my replying, "This *is* Reference."

A pause. "Hello." Another pause. "Hello, I want *Reference*."

Since this type of fruitless conversation could go on and on, I finally hit upon a satisfactory ruse. I always answered the main, circulation phone in a light, girlish, student assistant voice. Then, if the Reference Department was requested, I'd reply, "Just a minute, please," put down the phone, walk rapidly to the reference office, pick up the extension and say in a mature, no-nonsense contralto, "Reference Department." From that time on there was no more confusion among patrons phoning in. No doubt they thought the library efficiently well-staffed, while I found it fun to play two roles in the library's drama.

Limitations of time, staff, and book collections though there be, most librarians in most libraries are dedicated to finding the answers to the endless kaleidoscope of questions which come across their desks each day. Still, it's not always easy. How, for instance, would *you* answer these?

"Is modern marriage more for men?"

"Who was the only historical character who did not have a mistress when he was young?"

Chapter Seven

Please Don't Mumble

All too often patrons and librarians seem to be speaking different languages. This is more than just a case of the patron who is vague about his bookish wants or the librarian — most often a new, young assistant — who is guilty of showing off her knowledge of library shorthand: "Look in the cat. and if you don't find the book listed there, try the C.B.I." (Translation: "card catalog" and *Cumulative Book Index.*)

The most common type of communications barrier is caused by mumbled words issuing from lazy lips. It can be heard in the school, home, or general market place any day, but creates some uniquely amusing and embarrassing incidents in libraries.

In a West Virginia library a young man asked a question at the desk, whereupon the assistant working there led him to the shelf containing Western books. Shortly, the young man returned and repeated his question. Again the librarian directed him to the Westerns. Finally, in desperation, he came again to the desk and asked very slowly and distinctly, "Where are the REST ROOMS?"

What sounded like a real bathroomy book was requested of a startled Hawaiian librarian — "Passed Her Night in the Lavatory." But, she declares, by a sort of extrasensory perception developed after years of bridging the gap between school assignments and what follows "my teacher says," she was able to come up with the correct volume, *Pasteur: Knight of the Laboratory.*

More than one librarian has been heard to wonder whether all teachers mumble or all students wear ear plugs. A bit of both, I suspect. How else can one account for student requests such as these?

"I have to have material for a term report on a lazy fairy."
(Needed: material on *laissez faire*)
"I'd like 'Schoofer's Candle'."
(Needed: Sheridan's *School for Scandal*)
"I want a Greek biography of O'Henry."
(Needed: a "brief" biography of that author.)

Not all such boners are made by students by any means. It was the secretary to a prominent business man who called a library and asked to have the words of the song *America* read to her. The librarian brought a reference book to the phone and began to read slowly, "My country, 'tis of thee," when the caller interrupted.

"How do you spell that?"
"Spell what?" asked the librarian.
"That country — 'Tis of thee."

"Do you have anything about Bob Dwyer?" inquired a patron.
"Who is he?" asked the librarian.
Slight puzzled pause from the patron. "They make fences out of it."
What he wanted, it became clear then, was something about barbed wire.

A surprising number of telephoned requests for information arise from arguments between a couple of inebriated men. One librarian observes she often feels like asking if she gets a "take" if proved right, but finds that most of the time she has only bolstered the opposite side's contentions.

Music and clinking glasses could be heard in the background when a man called the Reference Room of the Carnegie

Library of Pittsburgh to ask whether Pittsburgh or Baltimore had the greater population.

"My buddy and me have a bet," he explained.

The librarian checked *The World Almanac* and reported that Baltimore was ahead.

"Good," the man chortled. "Would you please repeat that for my friend here?"

When the information was relayed to the second man, the librarian heard only gloomy silence for several seconds.

"Hmm," the bet-loser finally growled. "What's the phone number of another library?"

The Asian population explosion evidently concerned a befuddled better who phoned a Kansas library.

"We're having an argument," he announced. "Can Chinese women have babies in three months instead of nine?"

In December most libraries begin to receive requests for the names of Santa's reindeer. Knowing this, staff members of an Indiana library went about muttering, "Now, Dasher, now, Dancer, now, Prancer and Vixen!" just to keep the names fresh in memory. Sure enough, it was not long before that same old question was phoned in and a staff member was ready.

"Now, Dasher, now, Dancer," she began, when the caller stopped her.

"Wait a minute," he interrupted. "I have a bet with this wiseacre here about the next two names. Are they Mason and Dixon?"

When told the correct names were Prancer and Vixen, he said, very cheerily, "Oh, well, he wasn't right either. He said it was Johnson and Nixon."

Sometimes the mixed up one is more prankster than drunk. Such was probably the case with the questioner who called a Southern library. It was a busy evening with important questions to be answered when the Reference Librarian again took the telephone.

"What nationality is Bor Nosnhoj?" the caller asked, spelling it out.

Thinking aloud, the librarian replied, "It sounds like something or other spelled backwards."

Silence at the other end of the line — then hilarious laughter. "It is — Rob Johnson!"

★ ★ ★

Librarians as well as patrons sometimes have trouble making themselves understood. Speaking before a P.T.A. group one evening, an Iowa librarian reviewed several books on child psychology. Among them was *Just and Durable Parents* by James L. Ellenwood.

This librarian believed that she always enunciated fairly clearly, so she and her staff were more than a little surprised when at least a dozen of the fathers and mothers who had been in her audience came to the library and filled out applications to reserve "Just Endurable Parents".

Typical blush-bringing boners made by librarians are these.

A branch librarian reserved a group of books on rabbit breeding for a caller who, it turned out, wanted material on rapid reading.

When a woman phoned in, asking that *Scottish Chiefs* be renewed, an assistant made a note to "renew 'Cottage Cheese' for Mrs. Black."

Yet another librarian called the home of a patron to say that a reserved book was now available. Speaking to the husband, she informed him, *"The Ski Bum* is in."

"Are you telling me my wife is at the library, or do you mean a book?" he chuckled.

Embarrassing as it can be to make a mistake over the phone, it is infinitely more humiliating when a librarian's basic intelligence is challenged before a roomful of patrons, as witness this tale told by a male librarian.

A man approached the Reference desk and asked if the library had any books on "our treaties."

"What treaties did you have in mind, Sir?" asked the librarian.

"Our treaties. I don't care what kind."

"Well, do you mean our treaties after World War II, or what?"

"I don't know. I don't care when, just get me a book on our treaties. Boy," he exploded in exasperation, "I've never seen such a dense librarian."

By now all eyes were on the reddening librarian who was beginning to feel more than a little annoyed himself.

"Here," demanded the man, "give me your pad and pencil and I'll show you what I mean."

He scrawled angrily, then handed back the pad with one word enscribed upon it — ARTHRITIS. At the same time he said, "See, our treaties . . . "

While humans make mumbled errors, it sometimes seems that gremlins move among inanimate objects in libraries to cause ridiculous happenings.

After receiving several requests, *sotto voce,* for a book on sex supposedly in the library display window, a Canadian librarian decided it would be wise to investigate. He found that one book jacket had inadvertently slipped over the other causing a book entitled *Glove Making* to lose the G.

The staff of a large library in the South still laughs over this one.

Patron phoning in: "Does the library have *Green Hell*?"

Library switchboard operator: "Just one moment, please. I will give you that department."

In case it needs to prove that it is not really ruled by the Prince of Darkness, this same library can tell another story.

As two elderly ladies who had been visiting the library walked away from the charging desk, the librarian spoke to the guard. (Guards are employed by some large libraries partly to keep an eye on patrons who might try to escape with encyclopedias or other non-circulating volumes.)

Hearing the librarian's voice, one of the nice little old ladies turned to ask if she were speaking to her.

"No," replied the librarian. "I was talking to the guard."

As the ladies went along one was heard to murmur, "Isn't that sweet. She's talking to God."

Chapter Eight
Bookmarks and Overdues

"Who hath a book
Has friends at hand,
And gold and gear
At his command;
And rich estates,
If he but look,
Are held by him
Who hath a book."

The kinds of treasures visualized by poet Wilbur Dick Nesbit were the intangible literary variety. But another sort, real property, sometimes valuable in nature, is frequently found in books returned by absent-minded patrons.

With printed paper bookmarks, free of charge, available at most libraries (often supplied by local merchants), you would think that little else in the form of markers would turn up in books. Such is not the case.

Books are evidently read in every room in the house — the kitchen, the bathroom, the bedroom — while readers are engaged in other occupations, to put it politely. How else would you account for such marker items as nail files, bits of toilet tissue, and recipes? I once knew a librarian who discovered a much dehydrated fried egg deposited between pages. To my surprise — for this seemed like a once-in-a-lifetime happening — fried eggs were mentioned as markers by two other librarians from widely separated states. Warning, just in case somebody thinks this is a funny trick to be copied: there's no surer way of rousing the wrath of a librarian and losing borrowing privileges than by inserting a messy, smeary article in a book. And though a few might get away with it, most culprits are caught!

Candy and gum wrappers, popsicle and icecream sticks, even celery stalks, testify to the fact that eating and reading are often simultaneous occupations.

Bobby pins, hairpins, hair ribbons, a broken garter, family snapshots, religious articles, earrings, and charm bracelets all have found their way into books. So have pressed flowers, valentines, theater tickets, and bus transfers. And a librarian, checking her shelves one day, was startled when three beautifully pressed frogskins fluttered from the book she had in hand.

It was lucky for patrons who left in books . . .

    a dollar bill pinned to a gold safety pin
    two $20 bills
    a $100 bill (Confederate)
    a check
    a long string of trading stamps . . .

that librarians are generally honest people who will go to any lengths to trace rightful owners of property. Unmailed letters, with and without stamps, also turn up and are added to a library's outgoing mail.

While librarians and borrowers discovering currency in books appear, from all reports, to be scrupulous about attempting to return same, it would, indeed, be a soul with Spartan self-control who could refrain from reading some of the fascinating forgotten notes. Patrons leaving these do so at their own peril.

One man who had just finished reading a popular book remarked to a librarian, "I didn't like the book so much, but this love letter somebody left inside is a lulu!"

Another man apparently took his wife's desertion calmly. He sat down, read a book and used his wife's runaway note to mark his place.

And a wondrous document was discovered in a book by a New Mexico librarian. As nearly as she could make out from notations here and there, it was a list made out by an insecure young woman planning to go to school in Salt Lake City. "Insecure" it might be said because, in addition to listing groceries, school and household supplies to be purchased, she also reminded herself to find an apartment and look for a job. Unfortunately she made no notation reminding herself to take along the list, so the librarian envisioned her pacing the streets of Salt Lake City trying in vain to remember why she was there.

Forgetfulness is a conspicuous characteristic of patrons. Books leave libraries freely and easily; getting them back on time is another matter. Every librarian will tell you this is a major problem, and that many man- or woman-hours are spent in trying to retrieve library property and collect fines.

What might be called a classic example of this is cited by an Indiana librarian. A popular book with their patrons is *Stop Forgetting,* but its contents have been somewhat less than efficacious. To the date reported by this librarian, it had circulated nineteen times; eleven of those times it had required overdue notices.

Libraries generally send out printed overdue postal forms with the appropriate information thereon: title of books, date due, etc. Often two or three notices are sent before the book is either returned, given up, or more stringent measures taken, such as sending a special messenger. To their credit let it be said that most borrowers do reply to reminders by returning books or asking for renewals. Individual responses, however, range from the apologetic to that bordering on the apoplectic!

In one library where I worked it was policy to telephone the first notification of an overdue book. This was a task I dreaded when it came my turn because we were supposed to start on it immediately after library opening at 9 A.M. This was an hour, to judge from the curt responses, when housewives were yet to have that second cup of coffee after getting husband and children out of the house. In some instances, I'm sure, they had just settled down in bed for a second snooze. Very poor timing on the library's part it was from a public relations point of view!

When reminded of an overdue book, many patrons ask to have it renewed. Others request renewals before the expiration date. Often these requests are phrased in odd ways that cause chuckles, even though the caller's intent is serious.

"Can you renew a book *Before the Sun Goes Down?*" one wanted to know.

A man with a high, effeminate voice called his library to ask, "Could you renew *The Beast in Me?*" (*The Beast in Me and Other Animals* by James Thurber)

Perhaps the most startling renewal request came from a gentleman who brought a sack to the Circulation desk of a Florida library, plunked it down before the librarian, and asked that "these be renewed so I can keep them longer." "These" turned out to be two cans of beer and a pint of whiskey.

Some overdue books are returned on the sly. It is not at all unusual to discover a badly misplaced book minus its book card, indicating that a delinquent borrower sneaked it back on the shelf when no staff member was looking. Sometimes the borrower's logic as to where the book belongs is laughable.

A librarian, searching the shelves one day for a particular cookbook, found a book titled *Souping Up Your Car* shelved in that section.

A Texas Reference Librarian was arranging some out-of-order books in the first floor Reference Room. As she straightened and dusted a bit, she felt something tucked behind the tall books. Pulling out a few encyclopedias, she reached over back and brought out a small book belonging to the Children's Department which, incidentally, was located on the second floor. The book's title? *The Case of the Hidden Book.*

If the road to Hell is paved with good intentions, so, for most delinquent borrowers is the route back to the public library. They really meant to return those books on time — or at least to get them back eventually and pay whatever fine was charged. But, as in all areas of life, there are occasional careless or indifferent individuals who have no intention of keeping their library covenant. These, it is, who give librarians ulcers and bring about punitive measures.

It has been the policy of many libraries to send a special messenger employed by the library, or even the police, if a patron refuses to acknowledge repeated overdue notices. Most do not go as far as did the East Orange Free Public Library in New Jersey several years ago. They became the center of a nationwide controversy when they asked police to enter homes to look for long overdue books. It was reported that police, armed with search warrants, even routed delinquent borrowers from bed for this purpose. Later a judge issued warrants for the arrest of 38 persons found guilty of this misdemeanor.

While it is certainly legal to try to retrieve stolen property — and library books belong to all the tax-paying public, not to one individual — most libraries hesitate to take such stern measures.

Against the desirability of getting all books back must be balanced the need for good public relations in a community. In an attempt to solve both problems simultaneously, some libraries have an occasional "fine-free" day or week. The St. Louis Public Library found this worked out wonderfully well. About 4,500 books were returned in one day — not all "long overdues" I'm sure! Among these was a book taken out 44 years before.

Delinquent borrowers are found in all walks of life. It might surprise some people to learn that more books are stolen from the Divinity Library at Cambridge University in England than from any other of that University's libraries. But I have observed that the clergy seem to have quite as much trouble returning their books on time as any other folk. And I remember that a copy of the *Holy Bible* disappeared from the non-circulating collection in the Reference Librarian's office in Jacksonville, Florida. About a week after we discovered its loss, the book mysteriously re-appeared on the shelf. Apparently the reader got the religious message and repented.

Such was not the case with an 18-year-old fellow in Cincinnati. Alerted by the public library, police discovered that this young man had overdue books stacked clear to the ceiling in his bedroom. For this he was charged with "larceny by trick" and sent to prison for a short term.

When a librarian in another Ohio city phoned a patron's home to request return of a long overdue book the borrower's mother answered. The librarian endeavored to leave a message asking that the man get in touch with the library, but his mother protested, "He can't. He's in the Ohio Penitentiary." Oh yes, the name of the book? *The Power of Positive Thinking*.

Excuses, oral or written, delivered with returned overdue books are often ingenious. Sometimes this is because a patron hopes to escape paying a fine, but more often, I believe, it stems from a desire to be morally vindicated.

The following note from a rather confused borrower accompanied one overdue book.

"I was sure I returned the book, although it is likely I didn't. If the book was new and was about the 1900's or if it was an old brown book, I am sure I returned it."

A Canadian library had its troubles with a gentleman whose books were always several weeks overdue. Their time limit, clearly stamped in the book and on the borrower's card, was two weeks. However, the patron translated this to mean that if he could keep one book for two weeks, he could therefore keep two books for four weeks, three books for six weeks and so on. Since he usually took out a minimum of six books, it was often months before the library saw him again. Nothing they said could convince him that his reasoning was faulty. However, he would reluctantly pay the required fine; then the whole process would start all over again.

As mentioned earlier, responses to overdue notices range from apologetic to highly indignant. Here are two contrasting examples — both from young people.

"Dear Sir,

I returned the four (4) books. My Mother said I had to walk to the Library to return the four (4) books. But then I asked her if I could ride my bike. She said Okay, but be careful. So away I went. It was a long ride, but that wasn't your fault. It was mine. I admit it. I enclose the fifty cents penalty. Thank you very much." (Apparently this boy returned his books after library hours and deposited them in the outside book drop, a convenience many libraries have which makes it easier to return books at any time.)

Another library received this crotchety complaint:

"Note — in the future times (sic) try having a notice sent out before the books are two weeks late. I know you need the money, but letting the fine accumulate until it is almost $2.00 is ridiculous.

Sincerely,
Broke Teenager"

This points up a problem shared by all libraries. When should notice of an overdue book be given? The day it falls due? Several days after due date? A week? Two weeks? Librarians differ greatly as to when such notices should be sent. It must be admitted that in some libraries, especially small ones where the staff consists of one or two persons struggling to perform all library procedures, first overdue notices may not be mailed until a month after due date. At whatever intervals they go out, some patrons, like Broke Teenager, are sure to complain because they were not reminded sooner, while other patrons, usually the pillar-of-the-community type, are indignant because they were notified so soon. "Surely you knew I would return my books in time and pay the fine," they accuse in starchy tones, disdainfully placing the offending postal reminder on your desk.

Small wonder that to many library workers the whole routine concerned with return of overdue books is distasteful. Not only is it never-ending and often unrewarded, but it can subject you to insults, and may have an appalling effect on your social consciousness. When I've worked a long time on overdue notices, then met delinquent borrowers on the street, in a store, or at a social gathering, it was difficult to think of them merely as that pleasant Mr. Jones or friendly Mrs. West. Instead it was the man to whom you'd sent two notices to return F. Lee Bailey's *The Defense Never Rests* or the lady who owed $2.40 back fine on three books she'd hastily dropped on your desk when you had your back turned and were busy with another patron. As with St. Peter at the Pearly Gates, librarians in charge of overdue notices have little lists of delinquents indelibly etched on their minds. More's the pity!

Still, getting patrons to return books is an inescapable part of running an efficient library, so librarians will keep right on sending out overdue notices, lightening the task the best they can by enjoying some of the off-beat excuses given by the borrowers. For example:

A California library reported hearing a new excuse for not paying a fine. It seems the patron was in jail, and since it was a false arrest (according to him), he said he shouldn't have to pay the library fine.

Another California library sent word to a young lady that the book she had returned was badly damaged and she would have to pay for a new copy. Coming to the library, she protested, "How can you charge me for something that was an accident? I didn't mean to drop it in the bathtub!"

And finally, the most succinct excuse of any year, received from one young patron. "The reason I didn't return my book on time? My house caught on fire."

Chapter Nine
Merrily We Roll Along

Today's libraries-on-wheels attract eager patrons who often consider them a recent innovation. Yet the history of the bookmobile goes back quite a few years.

The great-granddaddy of today's custom built, shining steel beauty was born in the mind of a Maryland librarian, Miss Mary L. Titcomb. She was the first librarian of the Washington County Free Library in Hagerstown, Maryland — one of the first county libraries in the country, having begun operations in August 1901. By 1904 there were, in addition to the central library, sixty-six deposit stations dotted around the county. Some were in country stores and post offices. Others were found in creameries, at toll-gates and in private homes. Many were located in difficult-to-reach places where public transportation of that day — railroads and trolleys — did not go. Therefore, a horse and wagon was often used to transport boxes of books to these deposit stations. This, in turn, lead Miss Titcomb to wonder why a real "Library Wagon," one outfitted with shelves so that books might be displayed and from which they might be borrowed by householders along the way, could not be constructed. She put this question to her Board of Trustees and they heartily approved her idea.

So in April 1905 the plan went into effect with library janitor, Joshua Thomas, starting rounds with a book wagon which was drawn by two horses. From all accounts Mr. Thomas had a good deal to do with making this venture a success. Earlier, after fighting in the Civil War, he had returned to his native territory and, as a business, drove through the county buying butter, eggs, and other country produce to sell at the Hagerstown market. Thus, to quote Miss Titcomb from an early report, "he learned every road and byway in the County and was known by all the residents, unconsciously being prepared for this later undertaking. Absolutely loyal to the institution he served, a man of much native intelligence and a good fighter, he found a use for all these qualities, for the conservative element in the County was inclined to look askance at this radical departure in library service."

Though this particular wagon came to a sad end in 1910 when it was struck by a freight train at a railway crossing, the idea of bringing books directly to the people by means of a traveling conveyance was well launched. The Library would in time have another vehicle, this one an International Harvester truck, and other bookmobiles in succeeding years, each more modern and roomy than its predecessor.

Washington County Free Library, though it proudly proclaims itself "Home of the World's First Book Wagon," readily concedes that other libraries started bookmobiles at an early date, among them those in Hibbing, Minnesota, and Durham, North Carolina.

Early models of bookmobiles had a number of inadequacies. For some years books were shelved on the outside of the vehicles, with only wooden or metal panel doors as protection against the elements. These doors, of course, had to be opened whenever the book wagon was being used by the public, so only fair-weather service could be provided. And who, of a morning, can always predict the afternoon's weather? Its schedule was uncertain as was the personnel. At the Washington County Free Library, in the mid-thirties, the crew "was drafted from among those staff members who possessed drivers' licenses, and who happened to be at work at the time when the head librarian definitely decided that a lovely day might really be in prospect and perhaps the bookmobile should make its rounds after all."

Bumps, hollows, and grades on country roads were also a hazard. Even after new models of book trucks provided for inside shelving, not enough thought was given to engineering shelves so that books would stay in place under most conditions. Miss Marianne Brish told of her experiences on the Washington County Bookmobile in 1950.

"I began to wish about ten every morning that someone would decide to repeal the law of gravity. Washington County roads are said to be concrete reconstructions of Indian paths — presumably on the basis that whatever was good enough for the Indian is good enough for us. Unfortunately, most Indians seemed to prefer going straight up and over hills instead of around. Poor Delilah (the bookmobile) would charge determinedly at the hills, get about half-way up, and then, as Miss

Cooper, who usually drove, was changing gears, give a sickening lurch and a slight drift backwards while we held our breath and shut our eyes. Then, usually with a horrible, ear-piercing grind of gears and a mighty effort, she would plod forward. Meanwhile, the books on the back shelf had fallen off, one of the bags had burst, the closet door had opened and an umbrella had fallen out, usually on my head, but otherwise we were still intact."

What evolved from that first book wagon has to be seen to be believed. Today's largest, most expensive bookmobiles include such features as heating, air conditioning, fluorescent lighting, power generating plants, lavatory facilities, as well as all special library equipment necessary for good mobile library service. And now shelves are designed to slope to the proper degree so that books will not fall off in case of sudden stops.

Originally used mostly to bring books to sparsely populated areas, bookmobiles still do so. In certain parts of the country people come great distances, sometimes by horse or pony, to meet the bookmobile at a designated stop. Small country stores are often used as stopping points. At other times a bookmobile will pause at a cluster of homes to serve a few families, or visit rural schools, trailer camps, and even, so I've heard, an occasional county fair.

But today's bookmobile goes other places too. City library systems make increasing use of them. Urban stops include housing projects, shopping centers, parks, and schools. Some communities now use the giant-sized bookmobile as a branch library, parking it in one spot much of the time. Although expensive, a bookmobile does not cost as much as would construction of a permanent branch building. In some cases it may serve the purpose equally well.

Bookmobiles are found in many places in the World. The Gerstenslager Company, maker of the majority of bookmobiles, estimates that they have built approximately 2,825 such vehicles since entering the field in 1945. Today these traverse, not only the highways and byways of North America, but those of South and Central America, Europe and Asia.

Just as is true in other areas of our ever more automated society, technological progress in bookmobiles and the resulting changes in serving the public mean that a good deal of the unpredictable, folksy color of former days is missing. Several bookmobile librarians commented on this. They complained they no longer felt like "literary pioneers."

"Much of the spirit of adventure of the early bookmobile is gone," observes Mrs. Martha Healey of the Washington County Free Library. "We have become efficient and travel on exact schedules. However, a feeling of closeness to the patrons still lingers. When you see a half dozen people lined up along the road waiting for the bookmobile, you know you will hear county news and much enthusiastic book talk."

Some of the enthusiasm and importance attached to visits of the bookmobile is evident in this story.

On a New England route a housewife kept a collection of bookmobile books at her home for use by her neighbors. One day the bookmobile librarian found her greatly upset. When asked what the trouble was, the lady explained that her daughter was being married a week from Saturday to a man she — the mother — had never met. Belatedly the daughter had agreed to bring the man home so her mother could meet him, but she made the mistake of suggesting the wrong day.

The agitated mother repeated the retort she had made to her daughter: " 'Well,' I told her, 'You can't bring him on *Tuesday*. That's the day the bookmobile comes!' "

First visits to bookmobiles can be bewildering. Some children have hesitated about getting into a bookmobile for fear they will be given a "shot".

Similarly, an elderly Colorado couple struggled through the door of the vehicle (the lady was both feeble and plump) only to discover it wasn't the Chest X-ray Center.

And an elderly gentleman browsing through a Florida bookmobile for the first time appeared pleased with what he saw. "Have you any samples," he asked, "that I could give my friends to tell them about this?"

Then, of course, there is the question which puzzles so many small fry. What do you call the library lady in a book-mobile?

"Mrs. Bookmobile, will you please stample these books?" asks one child.

A small boy says to his even smaller brother, "Take your books to the check-out-lady." While another youngster drops his books on the counter with a cheery, "I'm cashing these in."

The feeling of working at a supermarket check-out counter sometimes afflicts librarians too. Whether stationed in a mobile library or a permanent one, working at a charging desk during rush hour can leave one exhausted and at the same time exhilarated that so many patrons have been served so speedily.

Young folks of all ages delight in bookmobiles. One library-on-wheels was visited by a very active young fellow of three. While his mother browsed, he investigated thoroughly all the features of the bookmobile. Having assured himself that the directional lights and the horn were in good working order, he turned his attention to the empty shelf under the counter. Curling up cosily on the shelf, he announced gaily, "Look, Mummy, I'm a book! Take me OUT."

In the closely confining quarters of a bookmobile it is impossible to avoid overhearing some amusing remarks made by the younger generation.

A 4-year-old, searching frantically for a "train" book, was offered one which he rejected with an anguished, "Oh, no! I can't *read* yet. That's much too duplicated for me!"

Two little girls had their heads together over a wild flower handbook when one was heard to exclaim, "Oh, I know that one. It's a Skunk-in-the-pulpit!"

A preschooler was perusing a book of Bible stories. All of a sudden she discovered a picture of the Cross and exlaimed, "Oh, my mother has that picture. The old RAGGED cross!"

On one bookmobile a child brought up a book to be charged which the librarian knew was much too difficult for him. She suggested he read her the first page. This he was unable to do, and reluctantly returned the book to the shelves. Later she found him with a song book and heard him mutter to himself, "I wonder if she'll make me sing one of these?"

Bookmobile librarians stock their vehicles with materials to suit many needs. With a book capacity of from 1,000 to 4,000 (up to 6,000 for a semi-trailer style), it is possible to supply a variety of tastes. However, there are often requests for additional books. For example, one trip might produce requests for books on opera, on making quilts, and on building cesspools. Such wants are filled, when possible, on subsequent trips.

Because bookmobiles by nature are informal places, and because they so often serve rural populations, there seems to be a personal, folksy quality to many requests. One bookmobile librarian revealed that they had been asked to find a flute teacher, to help shovel snow off a roof, to bring up hods of coal, and to find someone to stay free with a person dying of cancer.

But neighborly concern is a two-way street. If much is asked of bookmobile librarians, much is also given them. Assorted gifts from appreciative patrons have included lavender sachet, duck-grease cookies, a couple of garnet stones, and mulberry juice.

Liquid refreshments, it seems, are often pressed upon them. A California bookmobile had a stop adjacent to a fire station and, some years ago, the firemen provided the staff with root beer floats on warm summer days and hot coffee on cold days.

They were evidently more fortunate than the staff of another bookmobile who said that they were often offered, on summer days, six glasses of iced tea at six consecutive country stops with no restrooms between stops or aboard the book-mobile. Furthermore, the driver disliked tea, but couldn't bear to hurt patrons' feelings!

A Missouri bookmobile librarian tells how, at the end of a long day's journey over rough Ozark roads, she gave a book review for adults and a story for children at a small rural school in an isolated community. To her delighted surprise, she was presented with a corsage and a card signed by the eight or nine children, whose idea it was. "This," she says, "was an event to be remembered long after similar gestures of a proper, routine nature from more sophisticated women's clubs."

Although small tokens of appreciation may be graciously accepted by bookmobile librarians, the real rewards are more inspirational than material. To return to home base with shelves depleted because of literally book hungry people, to know that they and the books they dispense are meeting a real need in the community — this is what brings deep satisfaction.

Probably librarians of bookmobiles know, even more than most, that it is not only variety but humor which adds spice to life. Daily they encounter the unusual request and the unexpected remark, and generally remain unruffled and straight-faced. Yet, two librarians — one from the West Coast, the other from the East — were at first baffled, then highly amused by a couple of odd incidents.

A bookmobile checked on the list of books put aboard with a "voice-writer" machine. One of the men who drove the book-mobile and used the machine was very sloppy in his pronunciation of names and titles. When the librarian was playing back the record one day, she heard this title: *Sex, Indoors and Out.* Sure that a book by that title was not in their collection, she did some checking and discovered that the book mentioned was really *Insects, Indoors and Out.*

A man living in a motel on a busy highway in South Carolina checked a library book out from one of the bookmobile deposits. After months of trying to get the overdue book back through the usual methods, the bookmobile librarian decided to go to the motel herself and ask for the book. The title of the book was *Mary* by Sholem Asch.

Marching up to the lady desk attendant in the motel lobby, the exasperated librarian announced: "I've come to pick up *Mary*."

"You certainly won't get her," snapped the motel manager's wife. "She's my best maid."

Chapter Ten
A Potpourri of Patrons

"The cross section of users of a public library is as rich and varied with different types as in any other public place," observes one librarian. "We get the nuts, the down and out with no place to go, the students (serious and otherwise), the womans' clubbers, the crusaders, the religious, the pamphleteers, the staid business man, women playing the stock market, frightened youngsters who want to know marriage laws in neighboring states, desperate people wanting divorce laws or medical books. You know the list could go on and on, but you also realize that there is no stereotype of a public user."

It is this panorama of people — as well as a taste for books — that attracts and holds many to the library profession. Not all daily encounters are pleasant, but nearly all are enlightening. The librarian is entitled to enjoy witty remarks and happenings as well as to perform the worthwhile services which are implicit in her job. That she generally does so can be seen by the potpourri of patrons who parade through the following pages.

The Head Librarian of an Illinois library told this one. In a niche at either side of the double front door in their library are life-sized busts. To the left is Henry Wadsworth Longfellow; to the right, Abraham Lincoln.

A professor from the University often came to the library, accompanied by his two small daughters. One summer evening the 3-year-old broke away from her father's restraining hand and raced for the open door. "Here, where are you going?" demanded the father, trying to stop her runaway act.

The little girl spoke earnestly over her shoulder. "Up here, to see God (a wave toward the white-bearded Longfellow) and Jesus" (another wave, this time toward Abraham Lincoln.)

Youngsters are often sent to the library to take out books for their parents. (They come both with and without notes from home.) One little girl came regularly, once a week, always with the same request: "Please give me three books for my mother — love, ghost, and mystery."

Sometime later a small boy came to this same library to say, "I want a book for my mother."

"Love?" suggested the librarian.

"Oh, no," he replied. "She's had enough of that — she wants murder."

Possibly this boy's mother was related to the young woman in another state who asked to take out twelve books, explaining, "I don't want to run out of something to read on my honeymoon."

Most people never grow tired of reading about love and sex, no matter how old they are. A little old lady, who usually took out history books from her public library, one day selected a racy, modern novel and handed it , hesitantly, to the librarian. Noting the title, the librarian raised a shocked eyebrow and chided, "Why, Mrs. B., I thought you only read history!"

The little old lady blushed slightly, smiled sweetly, and replied, "At my age, honey, this is history."

Mysteries and suspense stories are popular fare in most libraries, but not with all patrons.

A lady, searching through the card catalog in her library, came across the following title entry:

Eat, drink, and be buried
Stout, Rex, ed.

She called for help in finding the book and the circulation assistant who came to her aid said to her as they walked toward the stacks, "I'm sure you'll enjoy that book. It's an excellent collection of mystery stories."

"Mystery stories!" exclaimed the patron, stopping abruptly. "I thought it was a book about diet."

Mysteries of one sort or another actually take place in libraries, but real-life ones, unlike those on the shelves, often lack denouement.

For instance, there was the incident of a gentleman rushing up to the Reference Librarian of a Louisiana library, waving a book he had discovered on a shelf in the circulation department. "Who returned this book?" he demanded. The book had been in the man's car when the car had been stolen several days earlier and he planned to do some detective work on his own.

While the thief was not identified by checking the library's records, the Reference Librarian conceded it was "nice" of him to bring back the book even though he kept the car.

At another library the police came looking for an escaped convict who was supposedly in the neighborhood. The librarian wondered what to do if he should come into the library. "I couldn't lock the doors," she explains. "We were open for business." She decided to call Mrs. S., former librarian of the branch, and arranged to have her call at regular intervals. If the convict was there, the librarian would say, "Yes, your book is here," and Mrs. S. would call the police. Mrs. S. called and called but the "book" never appeared.

From the way the branch librarian tells this tale, I think she was really a little disappointed that he didn't show up. She remarked rather ruefully that "It goes to prove the old saying, 'a library is no place to catch a man.' "

If car thieves and convicts make up a small proportion of a library's clientele, other lesser offenders are apparently more numerous. Several libraries mentioned them.

In California, a young man applying for a borrower's card couldn't seem to find any identification with his present address on it. Everything he produced had a different one. Then a happy thought struck him. Reaching into his pocket, he pulled out six tickets for traffic violations, all with his current address.

Similarly, a Florida patron applying for a card used a $34.00 light bill as identification. This cumulative account was stamped with a warning that the power would be cut off if the bill was not paid within eight days.

Poor risks like the aforesaid are admittedly part of the patron picture. But most library users are reliable and appreciative.

As the delinquent borrower subtracts from a library's stock, so does the patron who values his library's services often add to it. Numberless cartons of books are donated each year to libraries everywhere. True, quite a few of these volumes have seen better days. Some are dusty, mildewed, or hopelessly out of date because they deal with ever-changing subjects, such as the sciences. Quite a few bear tooth marks of mice. And because lack of shelf space is a critical problem in many libraries, the sudden appearance of a proud donor carrying armfuls of unsolicited books can cause suppressed groans among the staff. Since gift books seem to increase in spring and fall, one suspects that housecleaning as well as more selfless reasons motivate donations.

Yet, it's a good idea to accept gifts graciously, if conditionally, not only because this makes for good public relations, but because, quite often, usable books will be found. Duplicates of classics can help fill the need of students who are always clamoring — sometimes a dozen at a time — for the same title. And once in a while a carton of gift books will disclose a real gem, such as a volume of art with fine illustrations or an out of print book which rounds out the library's collection.

Gifts other than books are received by libraries. In addition to the always welcome monetary gift or bequest, groups of citizens sometimes donate funds for special purposes. For example, at the Hyannis, Massachusetts, Public Library, furniture in the Children's Room was purchased with money given by the Rotary Club.

In addition to money, libraries have received such gift items as electric percolators for staff rooms, tasteful paintings, models of ships and covered bridges, to name just a few.

When a prospective gift is slightly unusual, the donor might do well to query the librarian first. One librarian was asked, "Could you use a tree in here?" It developed, on further questioning, that the "tree" was an avocado plant, started from a pit, and fast outgrowing the lady's living room.

Librarians being human, it is not surprising that at times they harbor ambivalent feelings toward borrowers. The same patron who is full of hearty good humor may also voice annoying library clichés. I would, for instance, like to have a dime for every patron who has dumped a pile of incoming books on my desk, then announced, with obvious belief that he is uttering an original witticism, "Well, I'm bringing back your library!"

Then there are those patrons who call out loudly from the card catalog, "Miss, Oh, Miss, where can I find this book?" Busy with other patrons at the circulation desk, the library assistant has no time at that precise moment to dart to the catalog to answer his question. Worse yet, an impatient patron will sometimes tear the card bodily from the file and present it at the desk!

Speaking of impatient patrons, nothing sours a librarian's disposition faster than the borrower who requests a difficult-to-locate book, then does a disappearing act before she can return with it. The following verse printed in a staff publication is apropos:

> A Library is a happy place
> As long as patrons have the grace
> To ask for books that are in place.
>
> But then, we nearly always find
> They're sure to want the other kind.
> And when at last we find the book
> They often have no time to look
>
>   . . . Author unknown

In the category of patron complaints was this one received from a Southern library.

A lady, on being told by her branch librarian to look for material at the Main Library downtown, protested, "But I never go downtown except to buy a girdle!"

Libraries are often used for more mundane purposes than reading. A favorite cartoon of mine, by Ed Dahlin, shows three men — two with book in hand and one with hands folded —

sitting at a library table under a large "Silence" sign. First man to the second, indicating the non-reader: "He doesn't come here to read . . . he has a wife and nine kids at home."

While the man in the cartoon has a beatific smile and wide-open eyes, the quiet atmosphere of libraries has been known to lull quite a few souls to sleep. And not just unsought sleep either. In a library where I worked, a business man came regularly each day during his lunch hour, read for five minutes or so, then leaned back and took a snory nap for twenty minutes, came to quickly and left. I doubt that he was ever late getting back to his job.

Sleeping in libraries seems to be a universal problem. In Norwich, England (according to a UPI news item), City officials discussed a proposal whereby sleeping in library reading rooms might be prohibited.

A Canadian library had a problem of a different sort. One of the librarians, making a routine check in the basement study rooms, came upon a man heartily munching away on his lunch, while his uppers and lowers lay in smiling approbation on the table.

Most libraries discourage eating even with all teeth intact. But it still goes on.

Libraries make wonderful shelters in case of sudden showers. When inclement weather puts a damper on outdoor activities during the tourist season on Cape Cod, a Standing Room Only sign would come in handy in library Reading Rooms. Most of these refugees from rain read books or magazines but quite a few just sit and wait it out.

The question most often asked in libraries does not concern reading, it seems, but restrooms. One clerk at the Circulation Desk of a large library was so amused at the variety of ways the simple question was asked that she wrote a few of them down. Here is her list:

"Tell me, where's the toilet?"
"Where is the ladies' Lounge?"
"Is there a washroom here?"
"Where's the relief room?"
"Where does the man go?"

"Where is the comfort station?"

"Please, m'am, where's the water closet?"

"Where's the gentlemen's room?"

"Is there a powder room here?"

"The toilet's in the basement, ain't it?"

"Where's the pet(t)orium?"

"Where's the John's room?"

"Where's the head?"

"Where's the latrine?"

"Where's the bathroom?"

"Do you have a girl's room here?"

"Where is the ladies' toilet, please?"

"Is there a restroom upstairs?"

The answer cherished by the staff was that given, with a bow and sweeping gesture, by a foreign-born guard whose accent was rich with rolling r's: "To the rear of the structure, Sir (or Madam)."

Perhaps the most complete patron use of library accommodations took place in the Main Library of an Eastern city. Some years ago, a man and woman appeared on the scene and practically lived in the library from opening until closing for several weeks. They bathed in the restrooms; they ate their lunches watching the World Series on television. Noting the plainly pregnant condition of the woman, staff members discussed the possibility of having to deliver her in the first aid room. Then for two days the couple was missing. After that they reappeared, the woman no longer pregnant, and stayed around for another week. The staff never did discover what happened to the poor baby!

If this seems an unlikely story, it should be remembered that libraries are extremely conscious of being "free, public" institutions. As long as users do not commit overt crimes, break rules pertaining to books and fines, talk back to librarians, or bother other patrons, there are few grounds for asking them to leave. Their personal appearance, ethics, behavior, or beliefs are beside the point.

Since librarians have to put up with some rather odd characters from time to time, they might as well learn to enjoy such experiences if they can. It is evident that this next librarian did.

A man came up to her in the Reference Room one day and told her that there was one passage in the *Apocrypha* which would make the meaning of the whole world clear to him if he could find it. He didn't know any words in the passage or anything about it, so she brought him a copy of the *Apocrypha* and suggested he read it. He studied it a few minutes, then leaped up and shouted, "I have found it!" And rushed out.

He went out so fast she didn't have a chance to ask him what it was. Which, she says, was a pity. "I'd *like* to know the meaning of the whole world, too."

Then there was the man in another library who asked if they had a book entitled "The Assassination of God." A few minutes later, after checking the catalog, he came back to say, "Oh, I forgot. I haven't written it yet."

A certain library had an Indian who visited them frequently. At some time in the past he had lost a book called *The Vanishing Indian*. When he got rich enough to come into town, he always went first to the bar which was conveniently located around the corner from the library. After he had exhausted his money, he began to worry about *The Vanishing Indian*. So he'd come to the library and say he'd like to pay for it if he had any money, "which," remarked the librarian, "was a nice sentiment, of course, but unless the bar around the corner went out of business, I didn't think we had much hope."

He said he was king of all the Indians in the United States and Canada, and told one young assistant to bow down when he entered. Embarrassed, she went to the Head Librarian and asked what to do. The Librarian suggested she bow, so she did. Thereafter, whenever the Indian came to talk about *The Vanishing Indian*, he always singled out the young lady assistant — a development not exactly to her liking.

Some patrons are finicky about possible germs. A Mrs. T. insisted that one of the librarians pick out all her books because she didn't like to touch books which "Goodness-Knows-Who" had handled. They had to be thrust into a paper bag she provided for the purpose so that she could carry them to the health department in the Town Hall to have them disinfected.

Another patron, also evidently anxious about contamination, figured that the problem might have been licked when a new, big Recordak machine was installed in her library. Though this is actually a photographic type book charger, the lady inquired, "Does Recordak sterilize the books?"

There are always patrons who resist change. When the old globe lights hanging from a chain were replaced by modern fluorescent lighting in a Southern library, an elderly woman, who always dressed in black from head to toe, was furious. She claimed it was so bright it would ruin peoples' eyes. Day after day she came to the Reading Room and huddled, like an unhappy Mary Poppins, under an enormous black umbrella.

Just as small patrons use libraries more often than their busy parents, so, also, do the elderly make up a disproportionate number of library borrowers. It is easy to see why.

Older persons are often retired, have more leisure, prefer to stay home of an evening. Television, that other primary sedentary time-filler, is increasingly programming entertainment to appeal to the young, immature taste. Older people, because they can remember a day when neither radio nor television was part of their lives, can imagine doing without it quite well.

Furthermore, the elderly dwell in memories far more than the young. By rereading books enjoyed in an earlier day, they recapture old delights and renew acquaintances with old friends, fictional and factual. For all these reasons, older patrons constitute an important part of a library's clientele.

Many senior citizens are alert, intelligent, and a pleasure to know. If one can find time in a busy schedule to really listen to them, much can be learned about an amazing variety of subjects. And like the youngest patrons, they have almost a compulsion to confide in friendly librarians.

Normal, well-oriented persons though they usually are, a few because of senility, are pathetic if amusing.

An elderly retired college professor spent part of each day reading in his public library. One time, as he was leaving the building, he saw his shadow. Thinking it was a person, he bowed, held open the door and invited the "shadow" to come in. The library staff, while sympathetic, could not help chuckling.

The older, hard-of-hearing patron is sometimes a problem. A California library reported that twice the same little old lady was locked in the library at night. It seems she was using the microfilm reader, which is housed in a small dark room, so she wasn't seen by the staff. And being deaf, she didn't hear the "all out" call. Both times she called the police to come let her out.

There is a similar anecdote which may be apocryphal, it was submitted so often. Anyway, it goes something like this:

The telephone rings late at night in the house of the Head Librarian.

Small voice: "What time does the library open?"

Librarian: "9 A.M."

Small voice: "I can't wait until then."

Librarian: "You can come in THEN and not before."

Small voice: "I don't want IN. I want OUT."

Chapter Eleven

Beyond the Call of Duty

When Kenneth Tanke of Glen Park, Indiana, needed a live silverfish with antennae intact to replace one which had been lost from his daughter's award-winning insect collection, he contacted the Assistant Director of the Gary Public Library, thinking that some might be found skittering around the library. Miss Parks was doubtful, but called the Reference Department to see if anyone had noticed any silverfish lurking in the collection of old blueprints in the basement. No one had seen any in the recently constructed building, but an assistant there knew where she could find one. It seems that one had been making an appearance in her bathtub every day. Sure enough, that evening she was able to capture a fine specimen which she confined in a ring box. It was still very much alive the next day when Mr. Tanke stopped by the library to get it.

This episode (courtesy of the *Gary Library Bulletin*) points up the unusual lengths to which librarians will go to please patrons. No dedicated librarian is content with service that stops at the book shelf. She combines her talents, ideas — and often her idiosyncrasies — with others on the staff to come up with answers to all sorts of demands.

A heartwarming story from St. Louis involved another request. On an April Saturday several years ago, just prior to National Book Week, the telephone operator at the Central Library was asked for the home telephone number of Mrs. Kay Harnett of the Public Relations Department. The man on the phone said he just had to talk to her. Following instructions, the operator refused to give it to him, but he kept insisting. Finally she called Mrs. Harnett and through use of the open key Mrs. Harnett was allowed to hear the man talking. He sounded so earnest that she decided to find out what he wanted and gave the operator permission to be called. In a minute her home phone rang.

The caller explained that he was a cripple, confined to his home, yet an ardent baseball fan. He had heard that Satchel Paige, the famous Negro pitcher, (now included in Baseball's

Hall of Fame) was to be in town for National Library Week and was to speak at the Book and Author Luncheon. Stuttering with excitement, the man asked if there was any possibility of getting Satch's autograph on a baseball.

Mrs. Harnett decided that the difficulties were not insurmountable. All the man had to do was send the ball to his branch library and have it shipped down to the Central Library to Mrs. Harnett's waiting hand. The next day she lunched with Satch and the representative of Doubleday & Company, publishers of his book *Maybe I'll Pitch Forever*, and they got the desired autograph onto the leather. Back to Carondelet Branch went the baseball to the eager young man. His subsequent telephone call left no doubt as to his gratitude to the library.

Most acts which might be described as "beyond the call of duty" are not exactly earth-shaking. They do, however, go far beyond the automatic carrying out of library procedures.

As one librarian expressed it: "We put a special emphasis on being 'neighborly' in our attitude toward the public. It is fun and we enjoy it." One of her younger patrons plainly enjoyed it too.

Marlene, a 4-year-old doll with dark curls reaching to her shoulders, came to the library regularly with her mother. One morning when it was especially quiet in the library, the mother stopped to chat with the librarian, who, in the course of conversation, greatly admired the little girl's beautiful hair.

The mother smiled in rueful reply. Her daughter's hair was very difficult to wash, she complained, since with such long curls the shampoo always got into the tiny tot's eyes and made her cry. Thus, shampooing was an ordeal for both.

The librarian remarked that her sister once had a similar problem until she put a bath towel on the drainboard of her kitchen sink, laid her little girl on her back on the towel with her head at the edge of the sink so her hair fell away from her face. Then the job was easy.

Marlene's mother thanked the librarian and left. A few days later the library door flew open and a breathless Marlene dashed up to the desk where the librarian was sitting. Not stopping to catch her breath and beaming happily, she announced, "My Mommy . . . my Mommy . . . she wash my hair like you say!"

From that day on this particular young lady was a loyal friend of the Library.

While mailing letters left in books is a common library courtesy, a request received by a California library should certainly be classed as service beyond the call of duty. One rainy night a woman phoned and asked if someone at the library would please go out and search along the curb for some letters she feared she had dropped. Wet and smeared, they were found a half-block away by an obliging staff member.

At another California library a man slipped hurriedly up to one of the staff with an unusual request. He had locked himself out of his car and a policeman was helping him. Could they please give him a wire coat hanger to help open the car? The library rose to the occasion, granted the request, watched the patron rush out, and wondered ever after about the outcome.

A New York library tells of the time a man walked in, dropped some false teeth on the Circulation desk and asked if they could help him identify the owner.

Then there was the distraught lady who dashed into a library and appealed to an assistant: "Please zipper up my dress. I can't reach it and I'm on my way to a funeral."

The surprised assistant replied, "My hands are cold and may be unpleasant."

"That's all right," said the lady. "Better a little shiver than going to a funeral naked."

★ ★ ★

Certain library services, though not considered beyond the call of duty by staff members, still come as something of a surprise to outsiders. Many people think of libraries as places you go to borrow books and magazines. What they do not realize is that other materials such as pamphlets, clippings, maps, microfilm, and U.S. Government documents are also available for study and may sometimes be borrowed.

Most large libraries have an Audio-visual Department which handles films and recordings. An increasing number of smaller libraries dispense these on a less ambitious scale.

In one medium-sized library where I worked it appeared that the Audio-visual Librarian did, indeed, have a job beyond the call of duty in a most pleasant sense. I half-jokingly complained that while the rest of us were slaving away, filing catalog cards, puzzling over what classification to give a book, or trying to be tactful to difficult patrons at the Circulation desk, she was happily running new films in the empty basement projection room. She replied that this was all in line with her duty. By "previewing," she could tell the suitability of films to be lent to specific groups and recommend them intelligently to teachers, club chairmen, and other individuals. She also pointed out that she had responsibility for ordering worthwhile movies and returning those not purchased outright to the film depositories. Any way you looked at it, it seemed like an enjoyable job.

Phonograph records are dealt with in various ways. In some libraries small soundproofed booths similar to those in record stores are available to patrons so they may listen to music on the spot before deciding which records to borrow. Other libraries provide individual earphones or "audio drums" for private listening. Still others, while lending records, do not have facilities for playing them in the library.

Art lovers rate as well as music lovers. The Kalamazoo Public Library, Kalamazoo, Michigan, for instance, has a collection of framed reproductions of paintings which are available for free loan on a library card. Each year the library purchases only a modest number of reproductions but those they do buy are good, and representative of many styles, painters, and periods. Framed pictures are in such constant use that the library has had to make a catalog of snapshots of each of them and a set of color slides so patrons can select pictures for future borrowing. According to one woman I know, these are worth the wait. She is proud of the fact that each month a different picture hangs in a place of honor in her living room.

This same library has a Museum Department and offers, among other items, suitcase exhibits of museum articles, also loaned free on a regular library card. Director Mark Crum says that while he considers these services unusual, they are not unique.

Another Michigan library, that in Grosse Pointe, has a collection of tools which is maintained by a group in the city for loan to residents.

Other non-book items which libraries loan include toys, picture puzzles, children's games, chess sets, guitars, and easels for artists.

The Lynnfield, Massachusetts, Public Library also helps home handicrafters with knitting needles, crochet hooks, looms, and candle molds.

The Hyannis Public Library initiated a pattern exchange. Patrons brought in patterns which were in usable condition, then checked out others. Patterns for all types of garments for women and children were included in the collection.

Libraries generally promote their more off-beat collections and services through local newspaper articles and posters. Still, it's a good plan to inquire at the library to see if one's hobby or interest is currently being highlighted. Often, too, suggestions from patrons lead to new exhibits or services.

Some libraries have small auditoriums where they show films or give concerts — live or recorded — free of charge. Such places also serve as lecture halls where every subject under the sun is discussed. And meeting rooms are often made available to community groups for civic purposes.

Probably the ultimate example of how a library and the arts can be combined is the New York Public Library's *Library & Museum of the Performing Arts* at Lincoln Center. Here devotees of music, the theater, the dance, and all the graphic arts can find special collections and exhibits. In addition to several galleries, an auditorium, reading rooms, and a Research Library, there is a Children's Library with a "playhouse" which "is the setting of storyhours, film showings, record programs, puppet shows, concerts and dance presentations, all produced especially for children."

While other libraries content themselves with less elaborate setups, they nonetheless provide centers for numerous interesting events throughout the year.

The blind have not been forgotten by libraries. They, too, hunger for the knowledge, recreation, and inspiration found in books. Libraries such as the Chicago Public Library and the Denver Public Library operate special branches which provide Talking Books and books in Braille. Libraries which themselves do not have such collections may refer sightless patrons to centers which do lend them. For example: Recordings for the Blind,

Inc. in New York; Division for the Blind and Physically Handicapped, The Library of Congress, Washington, D.C.; or regional libraries cooperating in this latter program.

Thought has also been given to persons who, though not blind, have limited vision. Several publishers bring out books in extra large type and libraries often include them in their collections. Also worthy of mention is *The New York Times' Large Type Weekly* which publishes significant news and features from its regular paper in jumbo print. This may be found in some libraries.

Librarians are usually eager to serve handicapped patrons. There was, for instance, the Louisiana librarian who found a special volume on archaeology for a young polio victim in an iron lung.

A willingness to take extra time and care in selecting books for those who are bedridden or physically handicapped, it should be emphasized, is not considered by librarians as beyond the call of duty, simply a part of good library service. Indeed, a recent innovation along these lines is Home-Bound Service which serves either the individual shut-in, nursing homes, or both. Sometimes reading and listening materials are delivered by community volunteers, but increasingly this important task is assigned to a specially selected staff member who will do her utmost to make others aware that the program exists.

Since alcoholism is now regarded more as an illness than a moral defect, librarians should, I suppose, take a similar understanding attitude toward those in their library who display it. However, those of us who have witnessed incidents similar to that experienced by a Kansas librarian — and who hasn't! — find it difficult to consider it part of the normal, daily routine.

One cold night this particular librarian was working alone. A few of the regular patrons were reading when a new man wandered in. He fumbled around and finally sat down in a chair at one of the reading tables. A little later, the librarian happened to glance in his direction and discovered he had quietly relaxed, slid from his chair, and was completely under the table.

The readers were silently amused by the incident and watched to see how the librarian was going to handle the situation. She quietly went to the phone and called the police. They arrived, picked the snoozing man up by lifting him under the arms and carried him out of the library. It was obvious he'd had "one too many" to ward off the cold.

Students have altered the face of the library in the last generation. They now come in droves. A Virginia librarian says that their most unusual experience with these young people was when a couple, both still in college, brought their baby with them every night rather than pay a baby sitter. The climax came one night when they put the baby on one of the study tables and changed his diaper.

At a Missouri library the staff was surprised to see a middle-aged man dash into the building clutching a baby's bottle. "Where's the cold water?" he demanded.

After dousing the bottle at the drinking fountain, he turned to go. "It was too hot," he explained as he rushed through the door.

There are always requests to use the library phone. Many of them come from children. But one pretty young assistant was taken aback when a young man, determined to use the library's private phone instead of a pay phone for making a personal call, chucked her under the chin and coaxed, "You wouldn't make a cute fellow like me pay a dime, would you?"

P.S. She did.

Some thoughtless patrons, despite warnings to the contrary, underline passages in books as though they were personal property. Then must ensue, for assistant or clerk, a session with the eraser — surely an additional, unnecessary chore.

Another irritant, if you will pardon the pun, is beach sand in books. These little crystals are often discovered in books returned to coastal libraries. It's true that where a book goes after it leaves the library is nobody's business but the patron's, provided it's returned in good condition. But a day on the beach is as difficult for a gritty book to conceal as is sunburn on a patron.

An oh-so-true cartoon by Franklin Folger shows one of his middle-aged "Girls" choosing a book from the library, handkerchief in hand, and asking the librarian, "What do you think of James Gould Cozzens for a runny nose?"

It reminds me of all those patrons who, when they feel they are "coming down with something," dash to the library so they will have a good book to read before they succumb to bed and a fever of 102°. Often they will confide, while sneezing and blowing, that they had to be excused early from work because they felt so rotten. You, of course, are expected to be entirely sympathetic while they stand there, breathing into your face!

Only teachers are exposed to as many germs in such close quarters as are librarians. In Florida, a small measly patron bounded up to a Bookmobile librarian to show off his spots. And another boy, with a swollen face, gleefully asked, "Guess why I'm not in school today?"

Librarians just have to be made of sturdy stock or they would have disappeared from the earth long ago!

Despite assorted stresses and strains, some unpleasant happenings and difficult patrons, librarians generally take pride and pleasure in going beyond the call of duty to serve the public.

Such a one was the assistant who worked at the Registration desk of a library situated in a Jewish community. Sizing up the appearance of a man applying for a card, she felt he would be more comfortable speaking Yiddish, so she addressed him in that tongue. Afterwards, when she left the desk for a moment, the man turned to another girl at the desk and asked in perfectly good English, "Did she just get off the boat?"

Chapter Twelve

The Girls in the Back Room

For the most part the public has only the foggiest notion of what happens behind the scenes in libraries. Adult patrons are usually more sophisticated than the child mentioned earlier who, upon seeing assistants typing in a library work room, explained to her little friend: "They are writing books to put on the shelves." But even adult patrons make some surprising comments.

A grown woman, waiting at an unattended charging desk, was told by the returning librarian that her brief absence was because she — the librarian — had been in the cataloging department checking on an order for new books. "What!" exclaimed the wide-eyed patron. "Do you have to *buy* the books? I always thought the authors gave them to you." (Dickens and Shakespeare, too?)

At the top of the library's technical totem pole is the Cataloger. Professionally trained, she has taken library science courses which emphasize details of cataloging and classification of books. Her standing is equal with that of her colleagues in the Children's, Reference, and Circulation departments. In larger libraries, the more routine technical processes, such as preparing books for circulation, typing book and catalog cards, are done by clerical assistants. In smaller libraries the Head Librarian may also have to serve as Cataloger.

Today's tendency is to streamline the whole cataloging-classification process. Book classification numbers and appropriate subject headings are assigned in a central processing center. These are often based on Library of Congress decisions as issued in the *American Book Publishing Record* (Bowker). Printed cards incorporating this information are then made available to individual libraries. When the cards are received, only a minimum amount of typed information need be added to them before they are ready to be filed in the catalog for public use. In times past, every library had to work out this information for itself using the Dewey Decimal guide, then type each card in its entirety, so it is easy to see how timesaving such a service can be.

The central library in a regional library system, in many instances, will take on even the limited amount of clerical work involved in readying the pre-printed cards for library filing.

In 1971 a further development simplified much of the Cataloger's work. Under the Library of Congress' Cataloging in Publication Program, many participating publishers now print the catalog card information in the book itself. This is found on the verso, the reverse title page.

Helpful as are such methods, there is no immediate prospect of Catalogers being declared superfluous. Without their interpretations of general systems of library classification (Dewey or Library of Congress) to suit specific needs of local collections, books would be of far less use to patrons. When the whys and wherefores of library classification seem baffling, it is well to stop and think what a hopeless hodgepodge of books would result were there no logical systems at all to be followed!

Though Catalogers doubtless possess as keen a sense of humor as other librarians, few anecdotes were received from them. This is probably because they do not deal directly with the public and so many incidents which tickle their funny bone are "in" jokes. For example:

A book on goats and the care of their young (kids) came back from one library processing center classified as 649.1 (the number for *care of children*).

Similarly, though this happened at a main desk, not in a cataloging department, several librarians were puzzled about a request for a book entitled *Auto Conditioning* and looked in the 629.2 section (automobile classification) for it until they finally realized that what the person wanted was something on self-hyponosis.

Recent books from trade publishers are relatively easy to classify. Most are listed in one or another of the sources regularly used by librarians for this purpose. But some gift books are another matter. They may be out of print or from a limited edition. Often they are off-beat in subject matter and defy easy analysis. Others deal almost equally with several subjects. Two librarians debating correct classification of such a book can be as earnestly argumentative as a couple of fellows, each claiming merit for his favorite football team. The outcome may leave a librarian elated or limp, depending on whether or not she makes her point. But to an outsider it would all sound like so much gibberish.

One gift book which puzzled librarians, not over what to classify it but whether to classify it at all, turned up in a New Mexico library. Inside the front cover of a geometry book was stamped the following warning:

NOTICE: THIS BOOK WAS PUBLISHED BY MISTAKE!

To most library patrons, anyone working in the library is a "librarian." George was one of the best pages in a California library, even though he was only a 9th grader and barely tall enough to peek over a loaded book truck. An elderly patron, observing him industriously shelving books, muttered, "My, they do hire librarians young these days!"

While most librarians would consider this remark amusing, some — those overly concerned with their professional image — might also find it irritating. After all, with four years of college and an additional year to earn their Master of Library Science degree, it is understandable that they would not like to be considered on a par with a high school page! These same librarian-readers may also be annoyed that this book does not make a nice distinction between chief librarians, senior librarians, junior librarians, assistants, clerks, and clerical help. But there were two good reasons why this was not done.

First, contributors to the book did not, themselves, always differentiate. Persons mentioned in anecdotes were often simply labeled "librarians."

Second, stories came from dissimilar sources. Rural libraries with small staffs responded; so did large city systems having many branches. (Several have more than 1,000 staff employees.) Obviously, the professional quality of services offered the public is not equal in all libraries. But when it comes to happenings, both human and humorous, all libraries have them, and that is what this book is mostly about. So, although different *kinds* of librarians have been named (i.e. Children's, Reference), little attention has been paid to relative non-professional or professional rank.

As for the girls — and sometimes boys — in the back room, these staff members, though generally not visible to the public, deserve mention for the essential library tasks they perform. Accolades go, not only to catalogers, but to secretaries to librarians, typists and clerks, pages (yes, they pop in and out of public view), and book menders.

It seems to me that book mending is one of the most disagreeable tasks in library work. To be faced, day after day, with a huge pile of soiled, dog-eared, tattered and torn books needing repair, calls for the patience of a saint and the dexterity of an artist. Personally, I am all thumbs when it comes to mending. But the proficient mender, like the skilled surgeon, seems to know just where to put the patch that reconditions. Moreover, those menders I have known were cheerful on the job.

To be sure, there are commercial bookbinders who do a very good job of rebinding, but their services are not inexpensive; often a book will cost as much to rebind as it would to replace it with a new copy. So most libraries which utilize this service do so only for special books — those which are expensive, such as art books, or rare or out of print volumes. The rest are dealt with on the premises.

This doggerel rhyme, received from the Edmonton Public Library, Edmonton, Alberta, Canada, will no doubt strike a responsive chord with all book menders.

From the Book Mending Department

Thirteen members of the staff are we,
A small United Nations, you must agree.
Our work involves repairs on well-read books,
Such as Sue Barton, Tom Sawyer, and Captain Cook.
There are stacks and shelves of books we face each day
But each will be mended in its own good way.
Complete new binding is also done with skill and pride.
Our inner satisfaction we must not hide.
Although we work down in the hole,
Cooperation is our goal.

Our Motto Is:
     The difficult we do immediately,
     The impossible takes a little longer.

Chapter Thirteen

Coffee Break

Coffee break conversations in the staff room — or lunches in the lounge — are often spiced with anecdotes. As every librarian learns, a little bit of laughter makes those brought-from-home sandwiches go down easier. Refreshment, they discover, comes as much from shared experiences as from food and drink. To judge from the following tales, the stereotyped picture of a librarian as prim, proper, and humorless is broken along with the bread.

Upon returning from vacation, a librarian tackled the accumulated mail and messages awaiting her and was particularly intrigued with a business card which bore the pencilled notation: "Man called to see you about birth control." When the salesman finally showed up and was ushered into the office of this young, eagerly waiting librarian, it developed that his product was a method of bird control designed to keep pigeons and their products off the roof.

This contribution comes from a Southern library. A gentleman from "up North" frequently phoned long distance to find out about the weather in the whole southern area — at least so he said. However, the calls suddenly terminated when he learned that the "sweet young voice" with whom he had talked was married.

This same librarian answered the phone another time to hear a man ask, "Are you the tall, good-looking blonde?"

"No," she replied. "I'm the short, dark,pregnant one."

"Oh!" Click went the receiver.

An inter-library request slip marked with the book title *Lady Chatterley's Lover* somehow got into an envelope with the title showing through the address window and was then inadvertently sent to the local post office. Sometime later, it was returned to the library, stamped brusquely, "Address unknown."

Pregnant requests:
"Do you have any good biographies? I am pregnant and am trying to get my husband interested in something else."

A mother-to-be asked for a copy of *Great Expectations*.

When asked for a book on "child labor," the librarian correctly deduced that what was really wanted was a maternity handbook.

Found, the following note in a library's reserve request box: "Patron wishes to cancel her request for — Himes, *Planned Parenthood*."

A minister approached the main desk of a public library and inquired as to the location of books on sects.
Not hearing him too clearly, the librarian said quickly, "Oh, we keep them in the workroom behind the desk because they're always disappearing from the open shelves."
On discovering that what was kept in the workroom was books on sex, the minister remarked ruefully, "I wish books on religion could stir up so much interest that they needed to be kept under supervision."

A professor asked a librarian if she had a book called "How to Mate in Two Moves."
The librarian, not knowing that "mate" is a chess term, replied, "No, we don't seem to have that title in our catalog, but we have lots of other books on sex."

Some librarians — a small minority of those questioned — were reluctant to supply anecdotes for this book, fearing that they would seem to be poking fun at patrons. Said one, "I feel almost as though librarians, like doctors and lawyers, are bound to protect patrons from the fear of humiliation."

Now, it is commendable to respect a patron's confidence when the problem discussed is delicate, personal, and serious. Most librarians do. This is evident by the very small number of stories received which were in questionable taste. Those few which might have proved embarrassing to a particular patron who suddenly found himself in print were omitted. Librarians, like bartenders, barbers, and beauticians, are quite used to listening patiently to assorted tales of woe. They serve somewhat the same function as psychiatrists in allowing persons to let off emotional steam and to feel better thereafter. But, of course, they are not specifically trained for this purpose, and they do have many library duties to perform other than that of being a sympathetic listener. Still, most librarians sincerely try to help patrons in every way. No patron, confiding in a librarian on a really personal matter, need fear that his confidence will be betrayed.

But humor is something else again. Humor, like love, demands sharing. To pack away all the amusing incidents which happen in libraries into some secret box labeled "do not open," simply out of fear of hurting a hypothetical, hypersensitive patron, would be a great waste of wonderful material. Moreover, the healthy individual does not mind laughing at himself. He rather enjoys it. That being so, librarians must be in excellent mental health — so many sent in stories which were at their own expense.

One of the librarians in the Reference Department of a Midwestern library was asked to find some biographical information on William Faulkner and then telephone the patron needing it. She did so. But being rather overworked and pushed for time, as are most librarians these days, she got her tongue a little twisted. To her horror, she found herself saying in her most business-like voice: "Mr. Jones, I have the biological information you wanted on William Faulkner."

I had a similar tongue-twisting experience when a patron called the Jacksonville Reference Department to find out if there was a town in the United States by the name of Faugertus. Seems the telephone company had billed her for a call to it. I hunted in several sources including the *Rand McNally* atlases, all to no avail. Later on, when I called back, I must have been thinking of what I'd just had for lunch because I announced, "No, it is not listed and *Rand McNally* lists every hamburg." After a gasp from the patron, I corrected this to "hamlet."

A young Texas assistant answered the telephone one evening. "Is Mr. Roberts in the Library?" a man's voice asked.

"Wait and I'll see," replied the trainee-assistant. She then went to the reading room and paged aloud, "Is Mr. Roberts in the Library?"

The librarian who was in charge that night immediately realized that the assistant had been "taken." She chuckled, then whispered to the young lady that *Mister Roberts* was the name of a book. The assistant was so embarrassed she let the senior librarian answer the phone and explain that the book *Mister Roberts* was in circulation.

A nice looking middle-aged woman came into a library and inquired about stories concerning medicine. An assistant, being her usual helpful self, suggested a book titled *The Crazy Doctor*. Imagine her surprise when the patron, in applying for a card, wrote "Dr." before her name, and for her business address: "Psychiatric ward, County Medical Center."

While registering a new patron, a clerical assistant carefully printed after *Occupation*: "Lavatory Assistant."

Canadian librarians have their embarrassing moments, too. One, upon being asked for a book on RH factor (a substance found in blood), inquired of the patron, "Is he an English author, Sir?"

120

A dignified elderly French Canadian gentleman on failing to present his library card at the Ottawa Public Library was politely asked, "Monsieur, avez-vous perdu la carte?"

This question, repeated twice, elicited the same increasingly indignant reply: "Comment Monsieur?" which roughly translated means, "What are you saying , Sir!"

Too late, the embarrassed librarian discovered that far from inquiring whether the gentleman had lost his card, he was in effect asking him if he had lost his head! (Oh, the pitfalls of the idiomatic phrase!)

Librarians cheerfully admit their boners. But they also chortle over the snappy comebacks which sometimes slip out despite their best intentions.

A woman called to report that she had left a library book on a buoy in the Bay (San Diego Bay) and asked it if had been returned.

Librarian's comment: "By a seagull?"

With students standing four deep around the Reference desk waiting for help, one high schooler pranced up, pushed the others aside, and asked, "Where can I find George Washington?"

Without really thinking, the librarian blurted out, "Have you tried his grave?"

A gentleman patron, trying to be cute and confuse a pretty young assistant, smilingly asked, "Do you have a vest pocket edition of the *Oxford Dictionary?*"

"It altogether depends," she answered, "on the size of your vest pocket."

Despite the provocations which trigger such retorts, most of the time librarians retain their composure and play "straight men" to their witty patrons.

Teen-age boy: "I want a book for my sister. She's sick."

Librarian, pondering what to choose: "Is she in high school?"

Teen-age boy: "No, she's in bed."

Two patrons were overheard discussing author Albert Camus.

"He's sick," said one disapprovingly.

"No, he isn't," the other replied quickly. "He's dead."

Small folk, innocently unaware of the adult implications of their remarks, often cause their parents considerable embarrassment in libraries.

One little fellow, apparently on his second trip to the library, clung to his mother's hand as they approached the main desk. Then, spotting the charming lady behind the Recordak machine, he pointed at her and sang out, "I saw you with my Daddy last week!"

A California branch library was very quiet one evening. Then a mother and daughter arrived with neighbors — a father and his son. The foursome were excessively talkative and shared with each other their delight at finding favorite juvenile books.

The mother picked out some ghost stories. She told the man her favorites used to scare her. Her neighbor then remarked that he did not approve of scary tales, that his son was afraid of the dark and had to sleep with a light on.

The little boy, left out of the conversation, was incensed at his father's remark about his cowardice and said loudly enough for all in the library to hear, "Daddy is scared, too. He has to sleep with Mama."

Chapter Fourteen

A Changing Image

With the lively new concepts of library service have come changes in staff requirements. As we have seen, it is no longer enough just to be proficient in the details of library science — though this is an important qualification. Ideals of service to the public require that librarians use their imaginations, their individual talents, and be aware of the world around them with all its pleasures and problems. They must be alert, alive persons, concerned with both books and people. When these qualities are properly projected, librarians will have much less of an "image" problem.

One particular aspect of the changing librarian image has to do with sex. In the past, female librarians predominated to the point where most writers still automatically refer to all librarians as "she." But increasingly "she" is a "he."

Male librarians have image difficulties too. They have been labeled effeminate. And small children, who often fit librarians into a kind of mother image (as an 11-year-old girl expressed it: "The ladies are like a mother to me"), may be puzzled when confronted with male staff members.

One librarian found this out when he substituted in a Children's Library. Small patrons coming in appeared surprised to see him sitting at the desk usually occupied by a woman. Finally one of the little girls, after staring at him, went up to a woman librarian working in the area and asked, "If you are a librarian, what is he?"

In time, no doubt, male librarians working in any department will be taken as much for granted as male teachers.

Being classed as spinsters is a specter which continues to haunt female librarians. A survey conducted by the National Federation of Business and Professional Women's Clubs several years ago did nothing to dispel this notion. It reported that only 17% of the lady librarians interviewed were married.

Then there is that stern admonition made in *The Old Librarian's Almanack* by Edmund Lester Pearson: "Matrimony is no fit Diversion for the Librarian. The dissipations of Time, the vain Emptiness of Amusement, the general be-pesterment . . . harass the Librarian and woo him from his legitimate tastes." (Note that this observation was made about male librarians!)

Though probably written with tongue-in-cheek, the picture this maxim evokes is a persistent one — that of a cloistered individual, devoted to books but unaware of everyday life and unmindful of the opposite sex.

Public confusion as to whether librarians are more likely to be married or single was indicated, though perhaps unintentionally, in a note received by a certain librarian. It began:

"Dear Mrs. —

I hope you are Mrs. If not, I am sorry . . . "

At least one institution, The Los Angeles Public Library, decided to do something to counter the spinsterish image. Writing in the staff publication *Broadcaster*, Personnel Director Elliot Adelman made the following plea:

"We know of at least one candidate for employment who turned down a job with us, giving as the reason the lack of opportunity to meet suitable people of the opposite sex in the library. We maintain that this image of a library as an unromantic place is another ghost which should be laid to rest alongside the stereotype of the old maid librarian stamping cards. But we need facts to bury this phantasm, and we need your help to gather these facts.

"If you know of anyone who, while working for LAPL, met and subsequently married either a fellow employee or a patron, please notify the Personnel Office as soon as possible. The results of this survey will appear in a later issue of the *Broadcaster*."

The next issue stated that quite a number of answers were received. Seven examples were given: three library workers had married patrons; four had married other staff members. It should be pointed out that most of those who reported romantic results were either clerks, clerk-typists, or stenographers, rather than full-fledged librarians. Yet this survey is a step in the right direction. Who knows how many more well-qualified young people might be recruited to library ranks were other libraries to conduct similar surveys and publicize the fact that romance does sometimes bloom within book-lined walls?

Another way in which tomorrow's library image will change is by the increased use of automation. We are in the early stages of such a revolution now; some libraries already have pioneered in the use of computers. Among them: the Decatur (Illinois) Public Library; the Columbus (Ohio) Public Library; the Port Washington (New York) Public Library; and the Los Angeles Public Library. Quite a few college and university libraries have also installed data-processing systems or plan to do so.

However, most public libraries are currently automated only to the extent of using an electrically operated book charger and, perhaps, electric typewriters, or an automatic copying machine which will reproduce book pages, manuscripts, etc. Even such relatively simple devices can cause confusion and wonder among patrons.

In one library where an automatic copier had recently been installed, a young girl approached the librarian with a scribbled page from her notebook and asked, "If I put this in that machine will it come out typewritten?"

At another library having a photocopier, a boy was heard to remark, "Man, you could use that machine to copy money!"

And a lady at yet another library, wanting to have her book checked out, inquired, "Where do I have this book telecast?"

Actually, using television to help distribute books is not just a fantastic dream of the future. In Tokyo, Japan, for instance, there is a drive-in bookstore. When a customer drives up to the nine-story store, he can place his order without leaving his car. First, he indicates the title of the book wanted. Then the order is transmitted via closed circuit television. Although this store is huge, with perhaps one million volumes, it is said that the customer receives the book ordered in as short a time as two minutes!

Libraries of tomorrow may give similar service. In addition to drive-in banks, we may have drive-in libraries. And yet the thought is not entirely pleasing. For one thing, what would become of the delights of browsing? That, fully as much as the ability to find in a previously decided-upon title, is what attracts many patrons to libraries.

The videophone — a telephone with viewing screen so that caller and called may see each other — is still mostly in the demonstration stage. But if, in the future, it becomes widely available, librarians will welcome it, to judge from the remarks of a librarian from Washington state. She wrote:

"Did you ever try to explain how to read the phases of the moon and the accompanying diagrams over the phone — or explain how to fold the paper to cut a five-pointed star? Especially if you are like me and have some Italian ancestry that requires a few hand gestures! Certainly the phone with viewing screens will be a blessing to librarians. Maybe we can even hold up the pages of a book and let the patron do his own research. That'll be the day!"

Enthusiasm for automated libraries is by no means unanimous. To many librarians, adapting a library's procedures to data processing appears to involve a staggering amount of digitary detail. The familiar must of necessity give way to the experimental. Even librarians who converted some or many of their library routines to data-processing systems — and are pleased with the development — admit that study, trial and error, and much time was required before they could devise the best systems for their specific library. Also, staff members all had to go through a period of indoctrination while learning new viewpoints and vocabularies.

Several points about automation should be clarified. For one thing, it is not expected that all libraries, regardless of size and financial circumstances, are going to install complicated data-processing systems. What advocates of automation suggest is that many libraries be tied together by means of a teletypewriter network which emanates from a national or regional source and uses the most sophisticated and complete data-processing systems. Or they might — as some libraries already do — share computer systems with county or municipal governments, although this involves some problems as libraries generally require a more complex type computer program than do other city departments.

Then there is a distinction to be made between two different areas of library automation: (1) electronic equipment which sorts and makes available statistical data concerning circulation, cataloging, registration, payrolls, personnel records, etc.; and (2) reference or informational retrieval, which requires a more sophisticated set-up, usually connected with a centralized computer source, and is not yet in general use in public libraries. (It was demonstrated at the Library in the U.S. Pavillion during the 1964-65 New York World's Fair.)

When one studies all the predictions about tomorrow's automated libraries, one wonders if perhaps the image of the librarian may not change truly, but change directly from old maid to IBM! It does not take too great an imagination to foresee the day when we go to the library, push the proper buttons, receive a desired book by conveyor belt or slot, all without human contacts. Or we may ask our reference questions, not of a warm, concerned, living being but of a mechanized robot who is programmed to answer with computerized voice!

Proponents of automation assure us such nightmares will never come to pass. Use of data processing, they say, simply means that "routine operations are eliminated or vastly simplified" so that professional staff members will have more time to work directly with the public. Computers will speed up service but not do away with books or librarians. They contend that for too long librarians have been primarily "book housekeepers."

It's true that there are certain similarities between library routines and housework. (I learned this early on my first job when I was handed a cloth and told to dust books.) A typical librarian's day is fragmented, much like that of housewife and mother. This can make for frustration and inefficiency, of course, but it also provides variety and challenge.

I remember one particularly hectic, though not unusual, day when I was stationed alone at a circulation desk. A new patron was registering, needing to be prompted on how to make out his card properly. Another patron thrust forward a pile of books, part to be returned, part to be checked out. Change had to be made, as a fine was due on the returned books. At the same moment someone was clamoring to buy a picture postal card of the library and the only one remaining on the desk was soiled and bent. A quick trip for a fresh supply of postals, then back to the desk to give change and "thank-you" to purchaser of card. Immediately after came a search for a book card which had stuck to a book exiting with patron at front door. A hasty trip, hailing the patron on the sidewalk, to retrieve the book card.

As I sank into a chair during a momentary lull, I remarked to a passing colleague that if I were setting up a library school curriculum, I would insist on an intensive course in juggling. Tactile as well as mental skills could be profitably taught. To be able to make the hands fly in appropriate directions in rapid sequence, all the while having a sure knowledge of why each operation was being performed, was as essential as the usual courses in cataloging, bibliographical methods, or the history of libraries.

There is a strange impression held by many people that working in a library is a soft job. As a New Mexico librarian observed: "The most unpopular [patron] remark of this or any week is 'I wish I had a nice restful job in a library.' "

A New England librarian voiced the thought that "Although we're gradually getting away from the cartoon image of a librarian, I doubt if we're ever going to convince people that we earn our living. They all think it's a snap job."

Well, it's not a snap job, and if computers can really help make library work easier and pleasanter, more power to them!

Most librarians, however, are going to have to be shown that automation will really work to their benefit. Many have a fear as to what over-mechanization could do to those human contacts between patron and librarian which are at the very core of good library service. They will have none of the depersonalized image. Said a Public Relations Director of one large library, "I feel strongly . . . that the library should be shown more humanly — and less computer-ly (if you'll pardon the coinage)."

Let's hope that we — the librarians who contributed to this book and I — have done just that.

Finally, a bit of frosting in the form of a favorable comment.

A number of Pittsburghers adopted a new status symbol a few years ago when Carnegie Library introduced shopping bags bearing the library's imprint — for sale at the main library and all branches. One librarian heard a bag-buyer confide to a friend, "Oh no, I'm not going to *carry* anything in it! I just want my neighbors to see," she explained proudly, "where I've been."